Mathematics Olympiad

Class 01

A must have book for all
Olympiads & Talent Search Exams...

by
Niharika

BLoOM CAP
Bloom Cap Edu Ventures Pvt. Ltd.

Bloom Cap Edu Ventures Pvt. Ltd.

❁ Administrative & Production Office

'Ramchhaya' 4577/15, Agarwal Road, Darya Ganj, New Delhi -110002
Tele: 011- 47630600, 43518550

❁ ISBN: 978-93-25519-10-7

❁ PRICE: ₹100.00

❁ PO No: TXT-XX-XXXXXXX-X-XX

For further information about the books log on to
www.bloomcap.org

Follow us on

Preface

"Future belongs to those Who prepares for it today"

School Olympiads are National & International level competitions conducted by different Government, Non-Government & Educational Organisations with the purpose of making the children ready to face competitive exams. The challenging Questions asked in Olympiads motivate them to learn more & more and bring out the best result with improved academic performance. The Awards & Scholarship offered in Olympiads motivate children to aspire & strive for doing better and emerge out to be the best.

Maths Olympiads

Mathematics is an integral part of all competitive exams be it Aptitude or Commerce or Science. Maths Olympiads are meant to develop Mathematical aptitude in school students. They provide students with an opportunity to master their concepts and comprehend tricky questions effortlessly. Challenging Questions of Maths Olympiads encourage students to develop a logical approach to solve Mathematical Problems.

'Bloom Mathematics Olympiad Study Book Class 1' is a perfect resource to Study & Practice for Olympiad Exams and other National & State Level Talent Search Exams & Other Competitions.

Some Special Features of Bloom Maths Olympiad Study Books are;

- Chapterwise Exercises having different types of Objective Questions at par with the Olympiad Level.
- Detailed Explanation for each question.
- Olympiad Pattern Practice Sets at the end.

This book is prepared by Expert Panel with the utmost care, still if you have any suggestions regarding its improvement, then feel free to contact us at olympiads@bloomcap.org. We will try to inculcate your suggestions in the further editions.

Contents

Chapter 01

Numbers 1 to 100

1. Which of the following is not 6 in number?

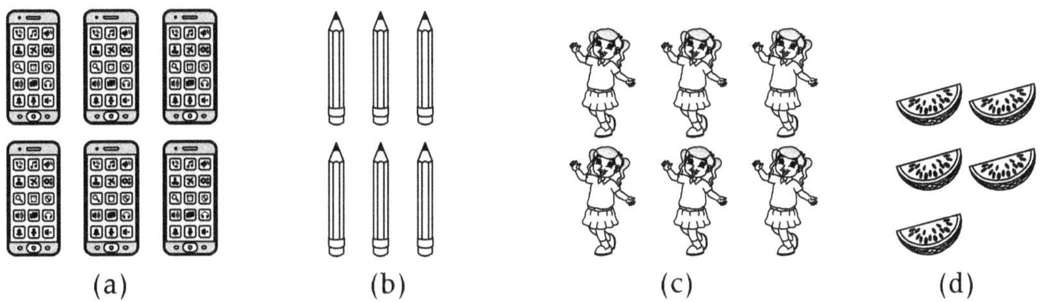

(a) (b) (c) (d)

2. Which of the following boxes contain 4 things?

A

B

C

D

3. Which of the following words contain 8 letters?

   (a) SHAPES (b) CALENDAR (c) MONEY (d) CIRCLES

4. Study the figures given below and mark the correct answer.

   (a) There are 4 flower pots and 3 apples (b) There are 4 apples and 4 flower pots
   (c) There are 4 apples and 3 flower pots (d) There are 3 apples and 3 flower pots

5. Which two figures given below have equal numbers of dots?

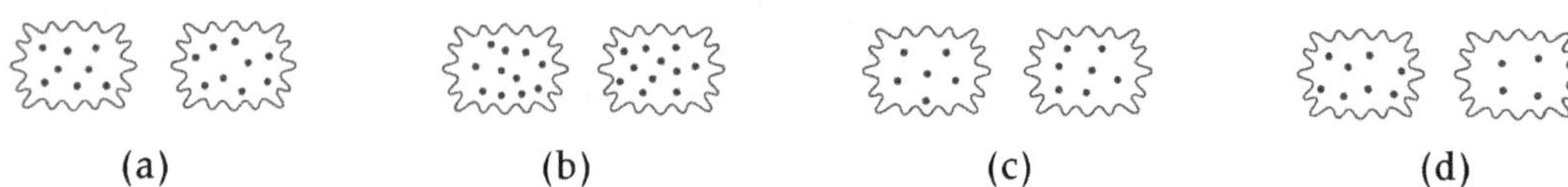

    (a)   (b)   (c)   (d)

6. Which two baskets have equal number of objects kept in them?

    (a)   (b)   (c)   (d)

7. Match the equal number of objects given in column I and column II.

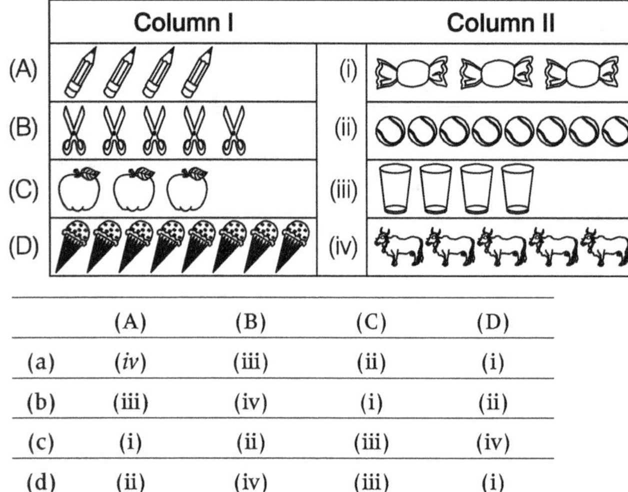

	(A)	(B)	(C)	(D)
(a)	(iv)	(iii)	(ii)	(i)
(b)	(iii)	(iv)	(i)	(ii)
(c)	(i)	(ii)	(iii)	(iv)
(d)	(ii)	(iv)	(iii)	(i)

8. Find the missing number in the given figure.

(a) 32   (b) 36

(c) 39   (d) 40

9. Write the missing numbers.

72		73		?		75		?		77	

(a) 74, 76   (b) 73, 77

(c) 76, 75   (d) 73, 78

10. What number comes in between in the given figure?

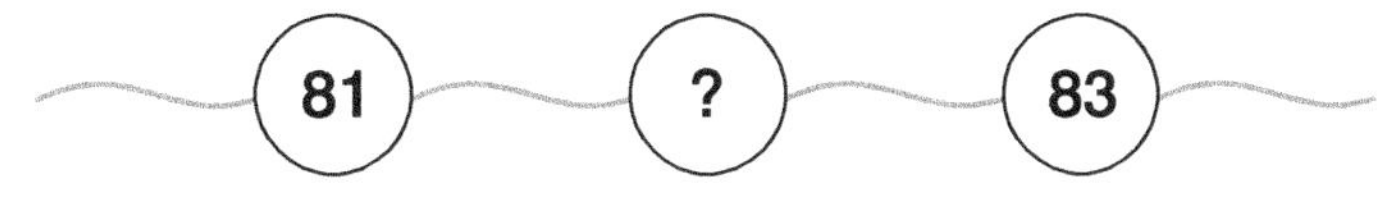

(a) 82   (b) 84

(c) 85   (d) 86

11. What number comes just before 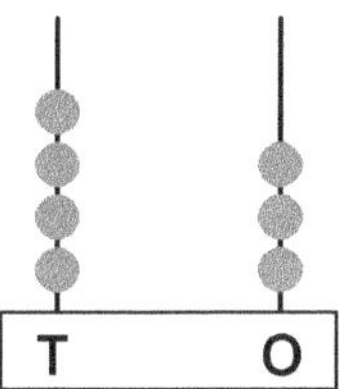 ?

(a) 69   (b) 71

(c) 72   (d) 68

12. When counting by 2, then which number comes just before 20 ?

(a) 16   (b) 18

(c) 22   (d) 24

13. When counting by 10, then which number comes just after 30?

(a) 20   (b) 30

(c) 40   (d) 50

14. Study the figure given below and mark the correct answer.

(a) Number of △ is equal to number of ○

(b) Number of △ is less than number of ○

(c) Number of ○ is less than number of △

(d) Number of △ is more than number of ○

15. How many tens are there in 43?

(a) 4   (b) 3

(c) 7   (d) 0

16. ⟨ ? ⟩ tens + ⟨ 9 ⟩ ones = ⟨ 59 ⟩
    (a) 4   (b) 5
    (c) 6   (d) 14

17. Tom saw a traffic signboard with a number written on it.

    What is the place of 8 in the number 78?
    (a) Ones   (b) Tens
    (c) Hundred   (d) Zero

18. The place value of 2 in 72 is ....
    (a) Two tens   (b) Two ones
    (c) Two zero   (d) Two seventh

19. 64 is same as ....

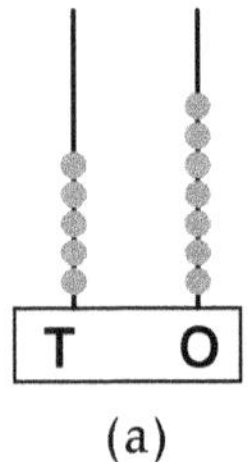
(a)

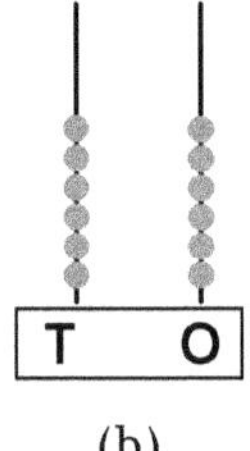
(b)

(c)

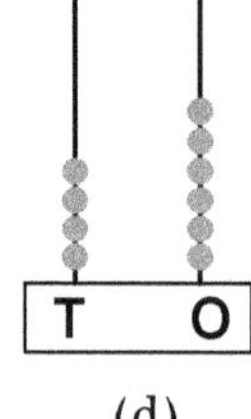
(d)

20. Which abacus shows the number that comes just after 20?

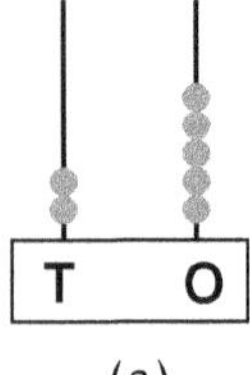
(a)

(b)

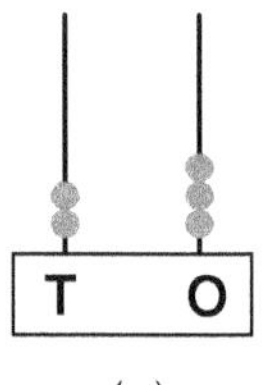
(c)

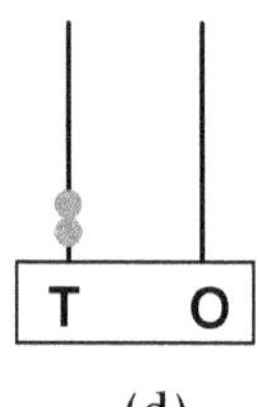
(d)

21. Which abacus shows the number that comes just before 20?

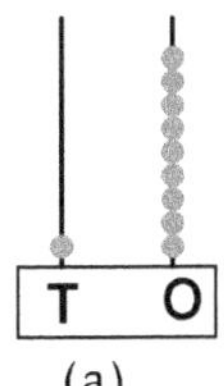  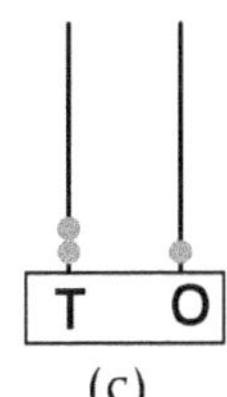 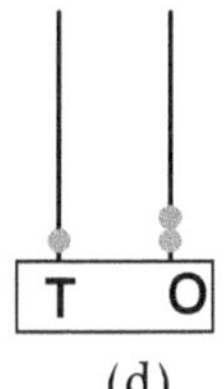

(a)   (b)   (c)   (d)

22. Which one of the following number is even number?

(a) 7   (b) 6

(c) 3   (d) 1

23. Count the number of parrots and mark the correct answer.

(a) Odd   (b) even

(c) Neither odd nor even   (d) Can't say

24.

A	B	C	D	E
14	25	9	36	19

Which block has the highest number on it?

(a) B   (b) C

(c) D   (d) E

25. Which balloon has the smallest number on it?

(a) 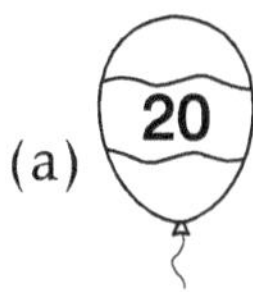   (b) 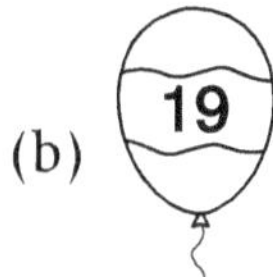   (c) 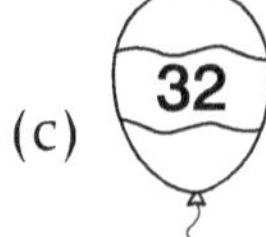   (d) 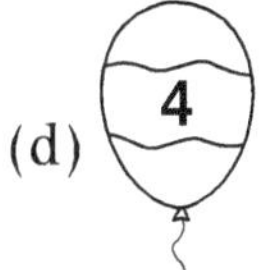

26. Arrange the following numbers in ascending order and select the correct option.

 32 10 49 51 17

(a) 49 51 32 10 17   (b) 51 49 32 17 10

(c) 10 17 32 49 51   (d) 51 49 17 32 10

Addition

1. There are ⬤⬤ blue balls and ⬤ black balls in a box.

   How many total balls are there in a box?
   (a) 7 (b) 8
   (c) 9 (d) 10

2. There are 🥭 mangoes in a basket. Rohan puts 🥭 more mangoes in it.

   How many mangoes are there in a basket now?
   (a) 8 (b) 9
   (c) 10 (d) 11

3. If 🍃 leaves are added to 🍃 , then total number of leaves are ....

   (a) 7 (b) 8
   (c) 9 (d) 10

4. Which number should be written in place of ?️ ?

   $$3 + 5 = \boxed{?}$$

   (a) 6 (b) 8 (c) 7 (d) 9

5. Which of the following is the correct sum?

   (a) $\boxed{6} + \boxed{2} = \boxed{8}$ (b) $\boxed{7} + \boxed{0} = \boxed{9}$

   (c) $\boxed{5} + \boxed{3} = \boxed{7}$ (d) $\boxed{4} + \boxed{4} = \boxed{6}$

6. Reena has 5 ice-creams and Sunita has 3 ice-creams. How many ice-creams does they have together?

   (a) 8   (b) 9   (c) 10   (d) 11

7. There are $\boxed{12}$ students in class I A, $\boxed{7}$ students in class I B. How many total students are there in class I?

   $$\boxed{12} + \boxed{7} = \boxed{?}$$

   (a) 18   (b) 19   (c) 20   (d) 22

8. Which two cards give the sum of 12?

   (a) 5 and 6   (b) 8 and 4   (c) 1 and 8   (d) 6 and 4

9. Count the balloons and mark the correct sum.

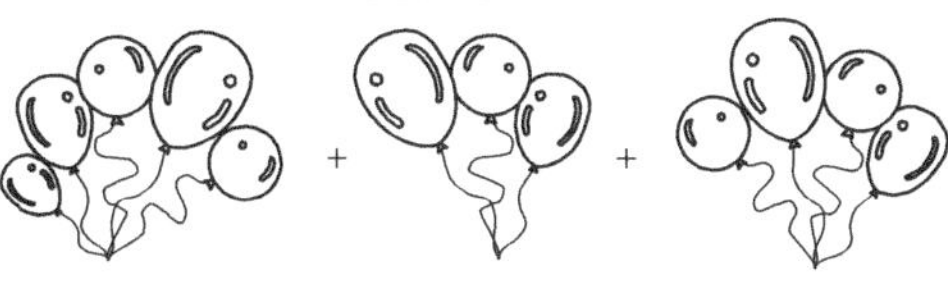

   (a) 10   (b) 12   (c) 11   (d) 13

10. Total number of cups, plates and spoons are ....

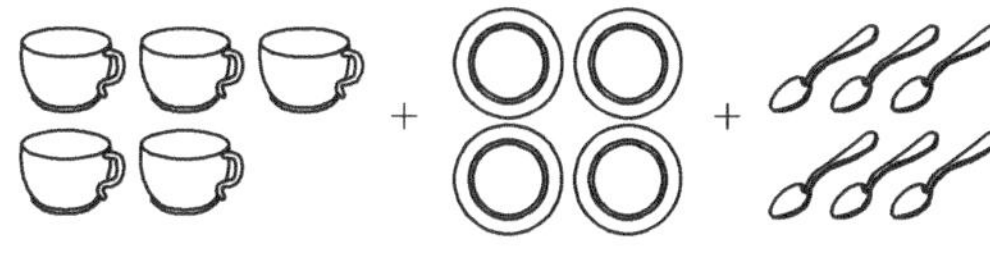

   (a) 3 + 5 + 7   (b) 5 + 4 + 6   (c) 6 + 4 + 5   (d) 2 + 4 + 7

11. Gauri bought 5 shirts on Monday, 4 shirts on Tuesday and 7 shirts on Wednesday. How many shirts are there with Gauri?

    (a) 14   (b) 16   (c) 18   (d) 11

12. Study the pattern and fill the missing term $\boxed{?}$ from the given options.

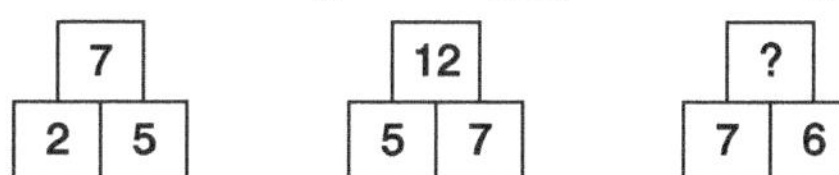

    (a) 7   (b) 13   (c) 15   (d) 9

13. Add the numbers on the dice and mark their correct sum.

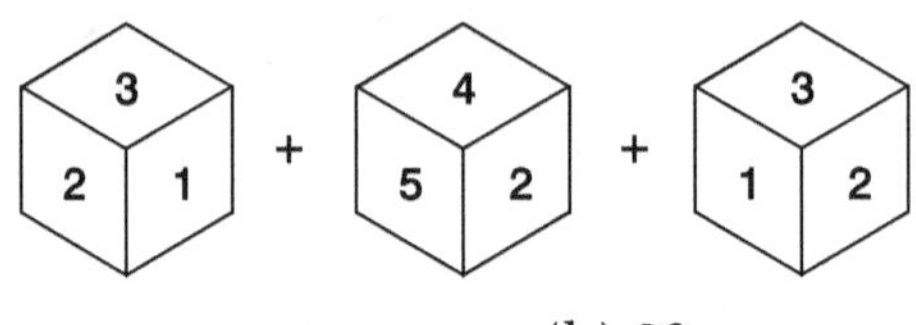

(a) 21 　　　　　　　　　　　　(b) 23
(c) 20 　　　　　　　　　　　　(d) 24

14. Choose the correct addition relation for the given figure.

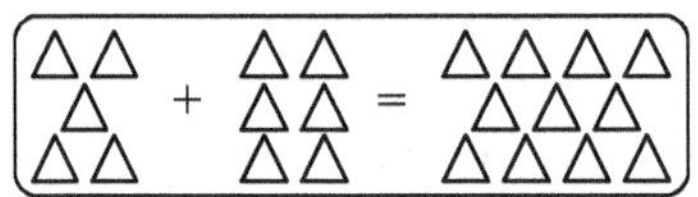

(a) $4 + 6 = 10$ 　　　　　　　　　(b) $5 + 6 = 11$
(c) $6 + 6 = 12$ 　　　　　　　　　(d) $3 + 4 = 8$

15. How many circles should be drawn in box B, so that the total circles in the boxes A and B becomes 15?

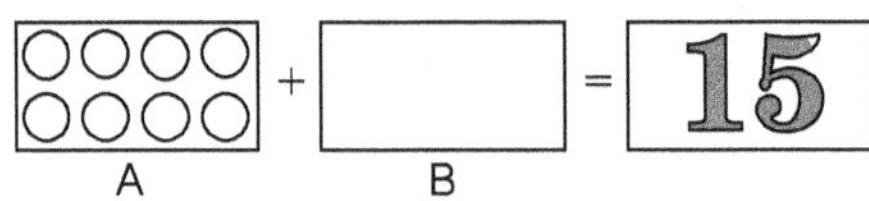

(a) ◯ ◯ ◯ ◯ ◯ ◯ ◯ 　　　　　(b) ◯ ◯ ◯ ◯ ◯
(c) ◯ ◯ ◯ ◯ ◯ ◯ 　　　　　　(d) ◯ ◯ ◯ ◯

Directions (Q. Nos. 16-18) Look at the given figure below and answer the questions.

16. How many flowers are there in Bag 2?
(a) 5 　　　　　(b) 7 　　　　　(c) 11 　　　　　(d) 4

17. How many total flowers are there in all the bags?
(a) 32 　　　　　(b) 30 　　　　　(c) 34 　　　　　(d) 38

18. Which two bags have the same number of flowers?
(a) Bag 1 and Bag 2 　　　　　　　(b) Bag 1 and Bag 3
(c) Bag 2 and Bag 3 　　　　　　　(d) Both (a) and (c)

19.

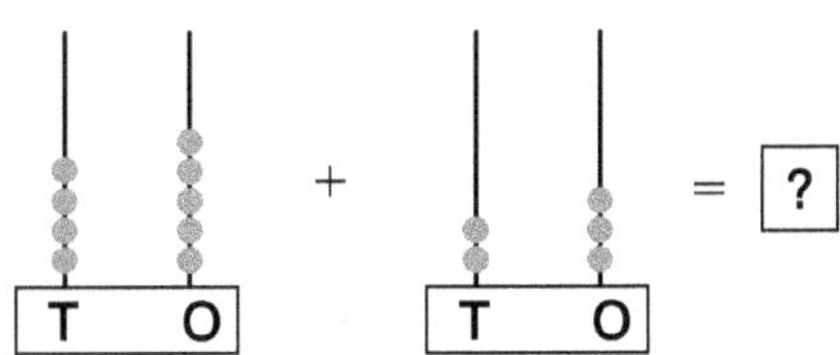

What is the value of $\boxed{?}$?
(a) 54   (b) 68
(c) 65   (d) 58

20. 23 $\boxed{+\ 14\ \text{is}}$ shown by which abacus?

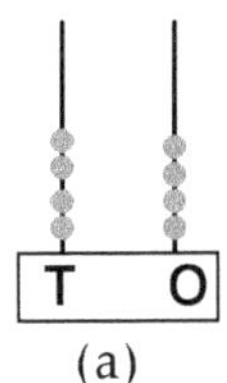   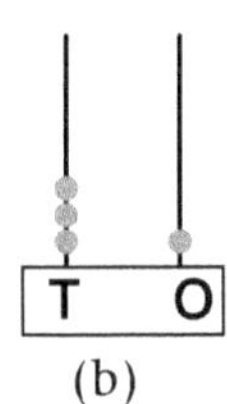   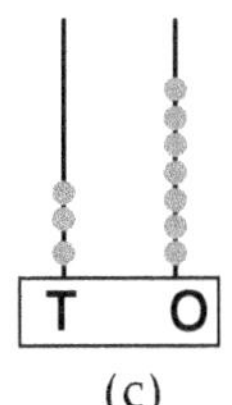   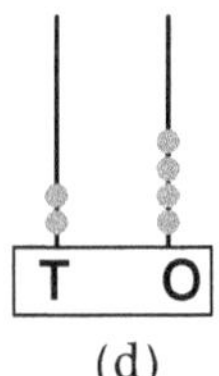

(a)   (b)   (c)   (d)

21. 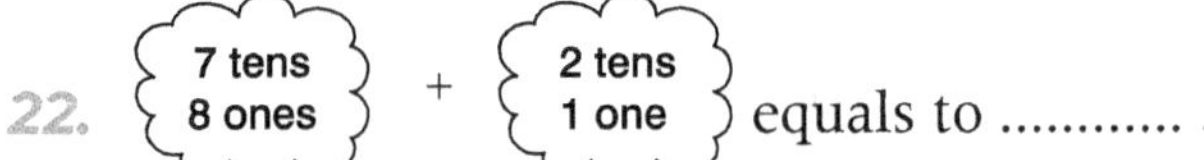 $\boxed{1\text{ ten }3\text{ ones}}$ + $\boxed{2\text{ tens }3\text{ ones}}$ = $\boxed{?}$

Which option will replace with $\boxed{?}$?
(a) 37   (b) 36
(c) 38   (d) 46

22. (7 tens 8 ones) + (2 tens 1 one) equals to ....

(a) 9 tens 9 ones   (b) 8 tens 9 ones
(c) 10 tens 8 ones   (d) 7 tens 0 one

23. If we add zero to 11, then what number shall we get?

$$11\ +\ 0\ =\ \boxed{?}$$

(a) 0   (b) 11
(c) 10   (d) 9

24. Rohan jumps 4 steps in one move. Again, he jumps 5 steps in second move. On which number did Rohan reach now?

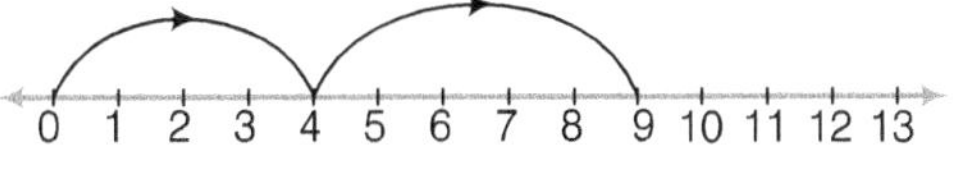

(a) 7   (b) 8
(c) 9   (d) 10

25. While playing Sumit takes 2 steps in one move. After the fourth move where will Sumit be?

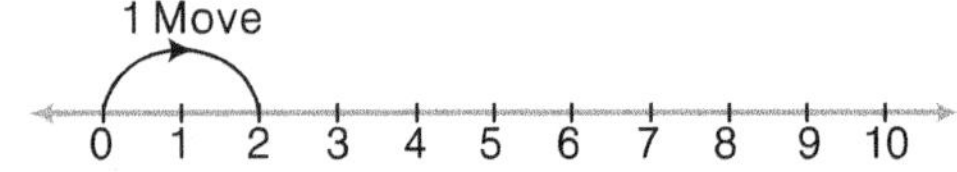

(a) 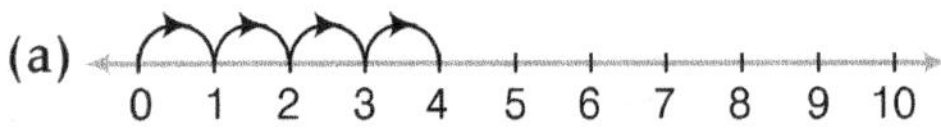   (b) 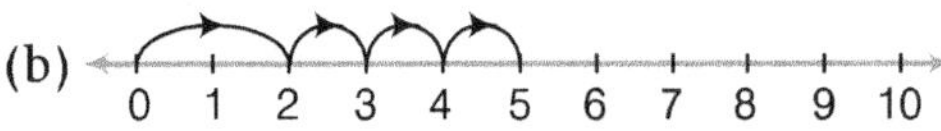

(c) 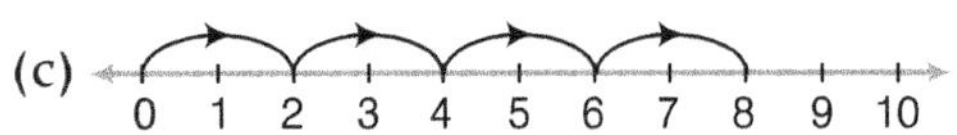   (d) 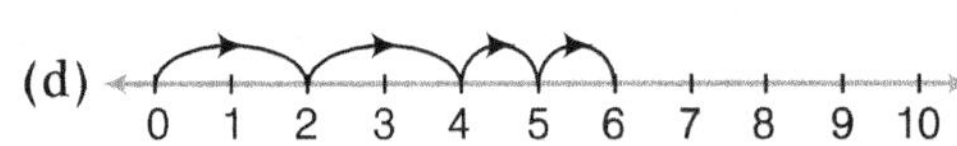

26. In which box " = " sign can be placed?

(a) $7 + 2 \ \square\ 4 + 5$ (b) $3 + 9 \ \square\ 2 + 5$

(c) $2 + 6 \ \square\ 3 + 4$ (d) $7 + 1 \ \square\ 1 + 4$

27. Which sum is greatest?

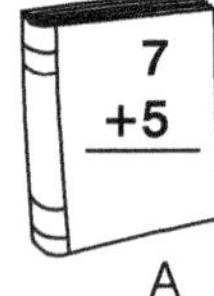

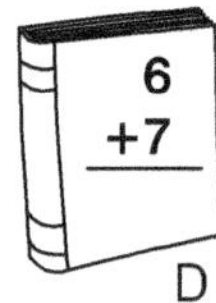

(a) A   (b) B

(c) C   (d) D

28. Arrange the given objects from greatest to smallest according to their sum.

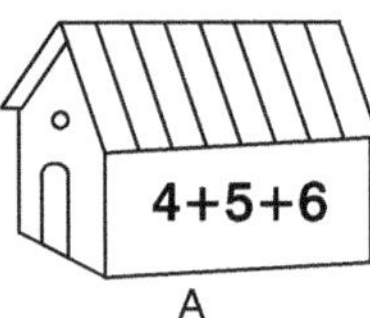

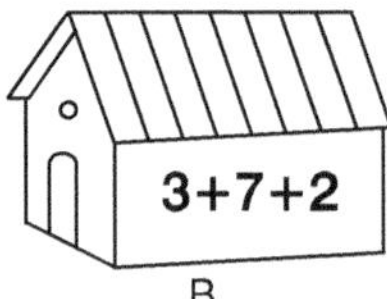

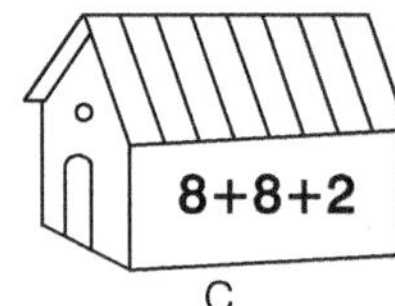

(a) A, B, C   (b) B, C, A

(c) C, A, B   (d) C, B, A

29. Look at the grid given below, where numbers are added across and down.

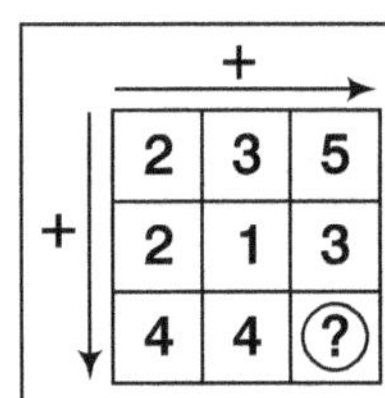

What number must be placed in ⟨?⟩ ?

(a) 7   (b) 6   (c) 8   (d) 9

Chapter

03

Subtraction

1. Find the difference between the number of balls in each box.

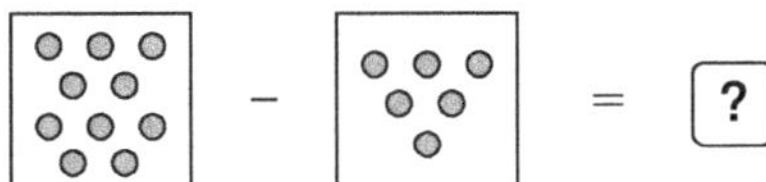

   (a) 3   (b) 4

   (c) 5   (d) 6

2. Choose the correct subtraction of leaves from the given options.

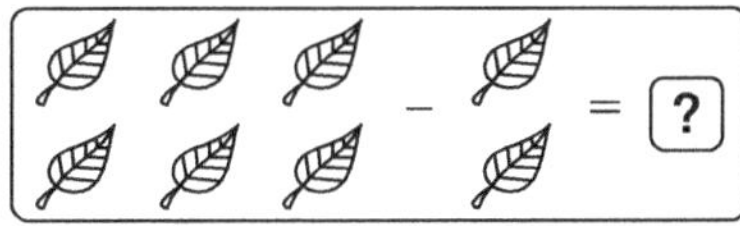

   (a)   (b)

   (c)   (d)

3. Salman had   flowers.

He gave   flowers to his mother.

How many are left with him?

   (a)   (b)

   (c)   (d)

4. There are ⚱⚱⚱⚱⚱⚱ flower pots.

   But ⚱⚱⚱ flower pots broke. How many flower pots are left?
   (a) 10   (b) 7
   (c) 3   (d) 4

5.

   How many fruits are left uncut if 3 fruits are cut?
   (a) 4   (b) 5
   (c) 6   (d) 7

6. How many softies should be crossed (✗) to show 4 softies uncrossed?

   (a) 4   (b) 6
   (c) 8   (d) 12

7. Ali had **12** ducks out of which **4** died due to some disease. How many ducks are left with Ali?
   (a) 7   (b) 8   (c) 9   (d) 10

8. Choose the correct number to fill in the place of ⬚ .

   48 − 12 = ?

   (a) 37   (b) 36   (c) 35   (d) 30

9. Which of the following options will complete the number bond?

   7

   (a) 9, 3   (b) 6, 1
   (c) 9, 2   (d) 8, 3

10. Which option given below is same as

?

(a) 

(a) 8 − 1   (b) 6 − 3   (c) 5 − 2   (d) 11 − 7

11. Select the correct subtraction from the options given below.

53 − 42 = ?

(a) 15   (b) 10   (c) 11   (d) 16

12. Ankit has 10 toffees. He eats 3 of them. Which of the following option shows the toffees left with Ankit?
(a) 10 + 3 = 13   (b) 10 + 3 = 12
(c) 10 − 3 = 7   (d) 10 − 3 = 8

13. A book has 66 pages. Vinya read 35 pages. How many pages are left to read by Vinya?

66   35

(a) 20   (b) 32   (c) 31   (d) 34

14. Which of the following option is a correct match?

(a) 29 − 14 → 20   (b) 25 − 12 → 37   (c) 37 − 11 → 26   (d) 22 − 10 → 21

15. Rachi has made some mistake while doing subtraction i.e.

79 − 54 = 28

What is the correct difference?
(a) 30   (b) 24   (c) 25   (d) 26

16. The value of SEVENTEEN − FOUR = ?

(a) THIRTEEN   (b) FOURTEEN
(c) FIFTEEN   (d) TWELVE

17. What should be subtracted from 9 to make it 4?

(a) 5   (b) 6   (c) 7   (d) 8

18. Which abacus shows $27 - 21 = 6$?

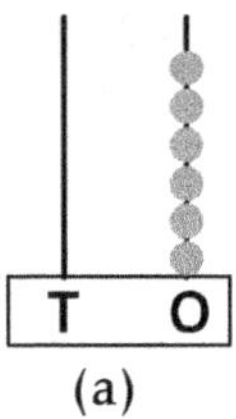 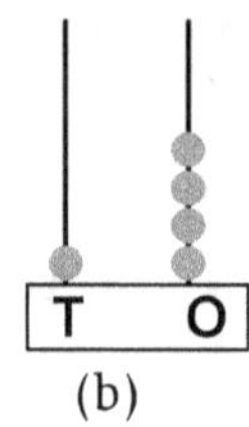 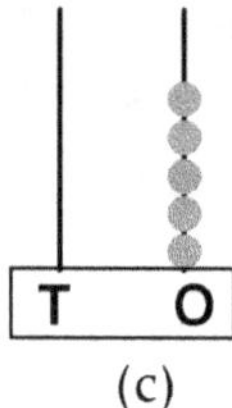 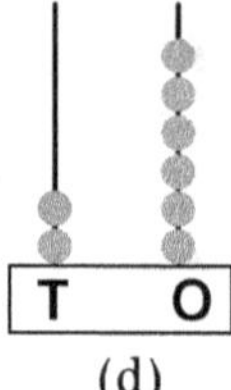

(a)   (b)   (c)   (d)

19. Which abacus shows $47 - 32 = 15$?

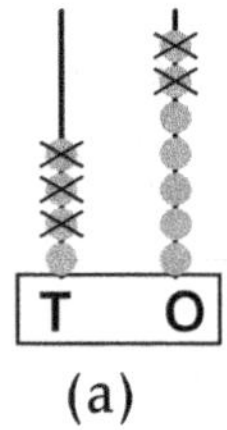 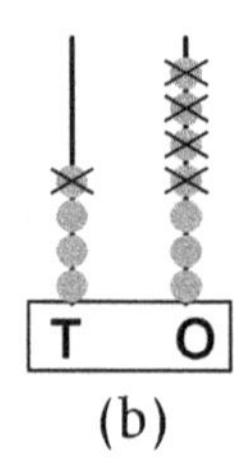 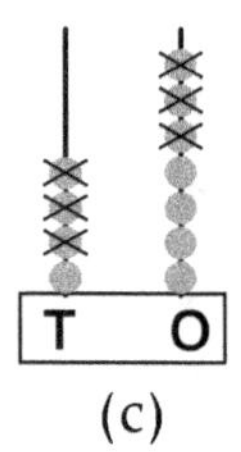 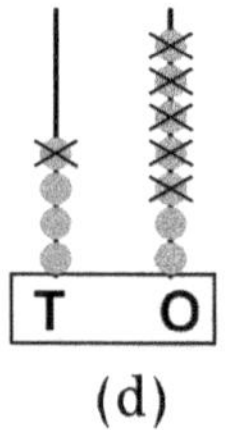

(a)   (b)   (c)   (d)

20. Ali jumps 9 steps forward. Again, he jumps 4 steps backward. On which number did Ali reach now?

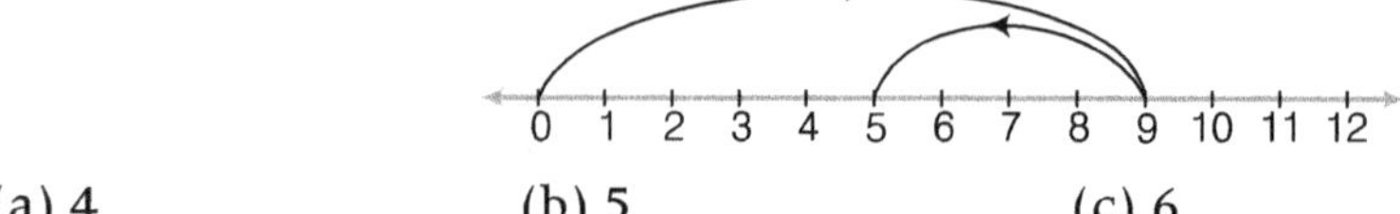

(a) 4   (b) 5   (c) 6   (d) 7

21. 3 less than 10 is represented by which number line?

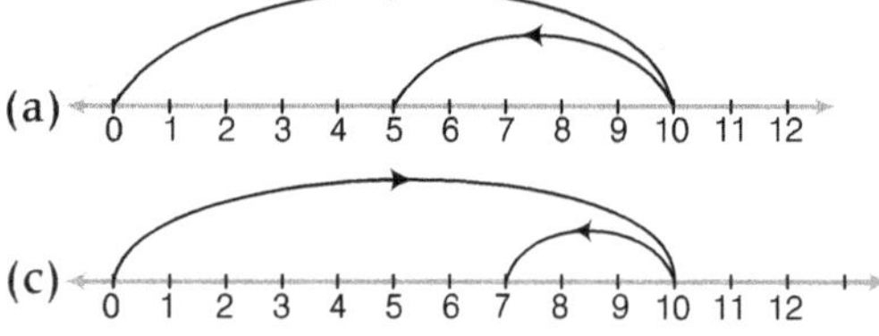 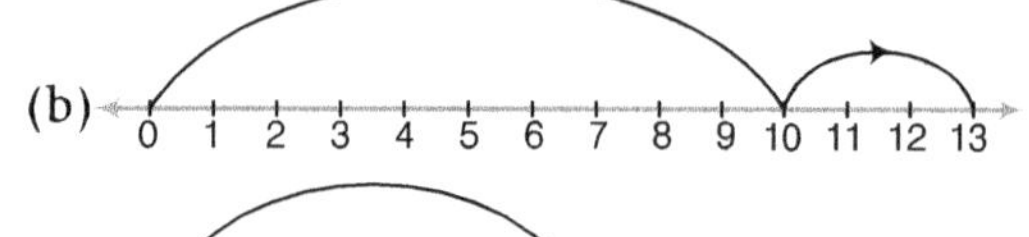

(a)   (b)   (c)   (d)

22. In a class, there are 84 students.

42 of them are  .

How many are there in a class?

(a) 42   (b) 60   (c) 40   (d) 24

23. If  △ = 15 and ▯ = 12, then which of the following shows △ - ▯ ?

(a) 2   (b) 3

(c) 4   (d) 5

24. How many more balls are needed such that the number of bats and balls become equal?

(a) 7   (b) 5

(c) 12   (d) 17

25. 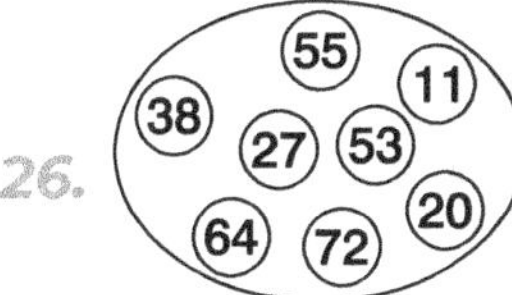 9 tens 3 ones − 6 tens 2 ones = { ? }

Choose the correct option for { ? }.

(a) 3 tens 1 one   (b) 4 tens 2 ones
(c) 1 one 3 tens   (d) 3 tens 7 ones

26.

Difference between the greatest and the smallest numbers in the above collection is ....

(a) 53   (b) 26

(c) 61   (d) 63

27. Number are subtracted across and down in the given grid.

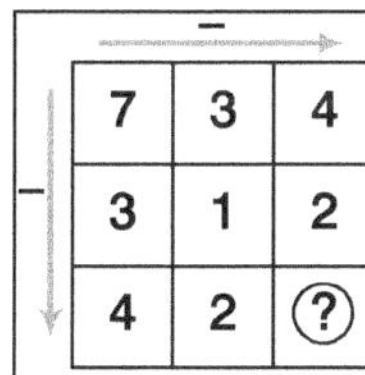

7	3	4
3	1	2
4	2	(?)

What number must be placed in (?) ?

(a) 8   (b) 6

(c) 2   (d) 1

Measurement

1. Which is the longest key?

   (a) 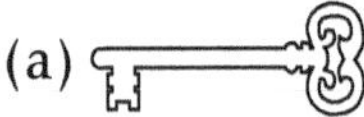   (b) 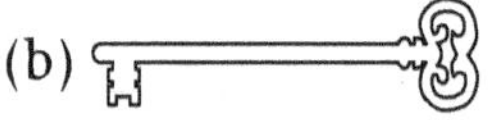   (c) 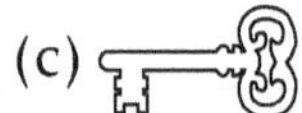   (d) 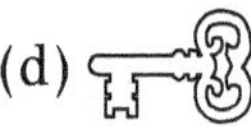

2. Which ice-cream is the biggest?

   (a) 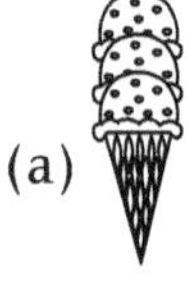   (b) 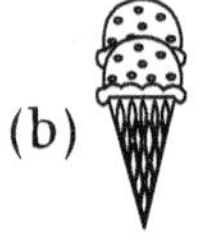   (c) 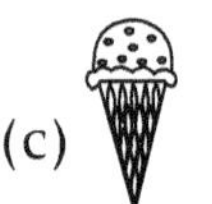   (d) 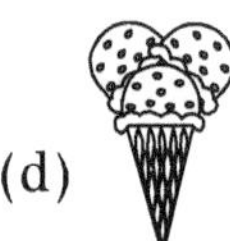

3. Which kite has the shortest tail?

   (a) 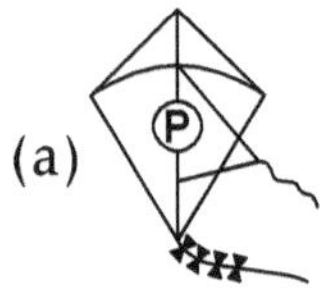   (b) 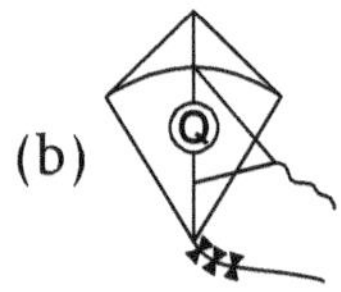

   (c) 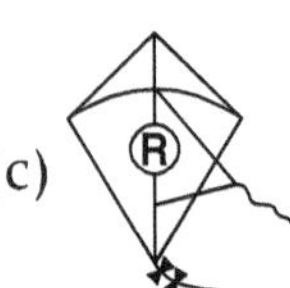   (d) 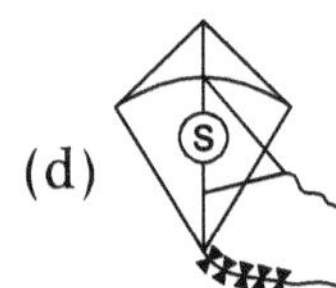

4. Which hammer is longer than hammer R?

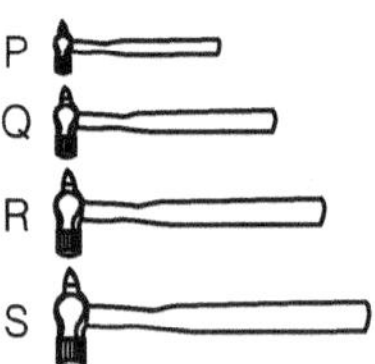

   (a) P   (b) Q   (c) S   (d) Both P and Q

5. The length of the ladder is .... metres.

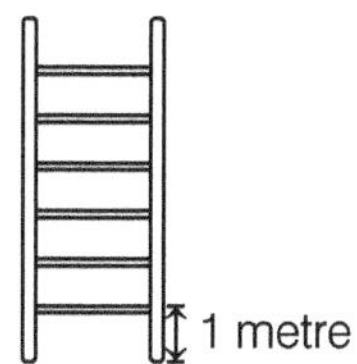

(a) 6 (b) 7 (c) 8 (d) 9

6. Length of the pencil is ....

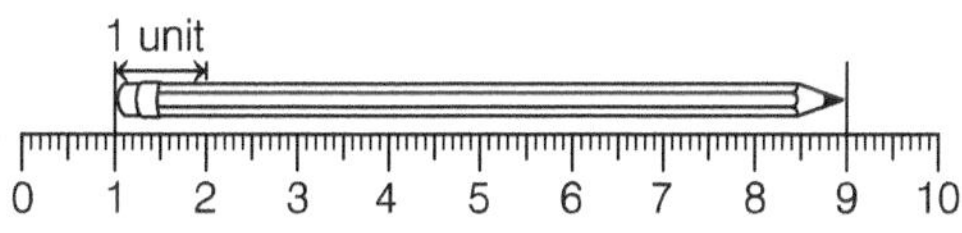

(a) 8 units (b) 9 units (c) 10 units (d) 7 units

Directions (Q. Nos. 7-10) Answer the questions based on the given figure.

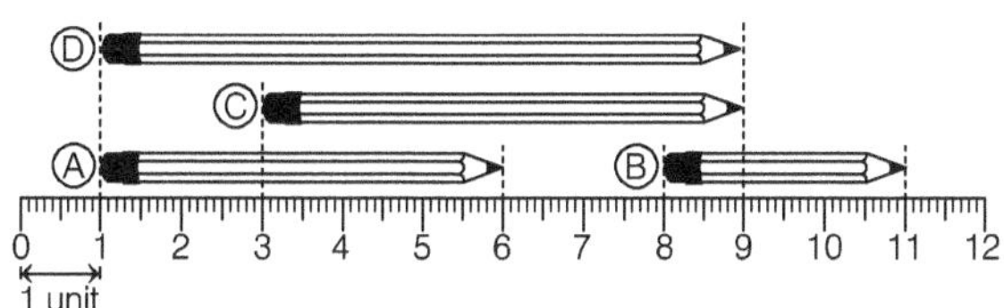

7. Which is the longest pencil?
(a) A (b) B (c) C (d) D

8. Which is the smallest pencil?
(a) A (b) B (c) C (d) D

9. Pencil B is shorter than pencil C by .... units.
(a) 2 (b) 3 (c) 4 (d) 5

10. The length of pencil D is .... units.
(a) 7 (b) 8 (c) 9 (d) 10

11. Which butterfly is at the greatest distance from the wall?

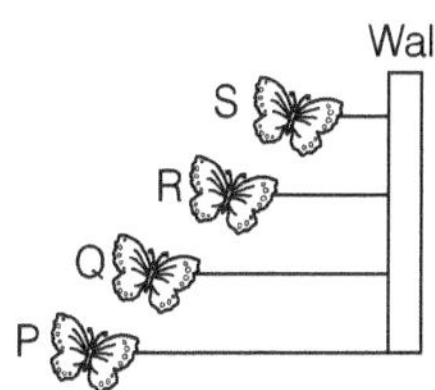

(a) P (b) Q (c) R (d) S

12. Distance between tree A and tree B is .... metre.

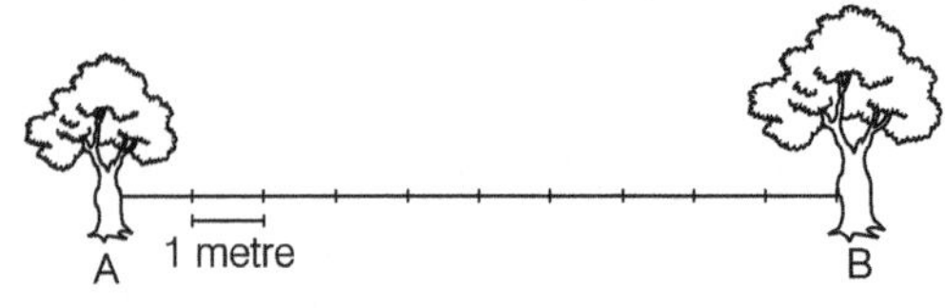

(a) 10   (b) 11   (c) 9   (d) 8

13. Seema has two pieces of rope measuring 5 metres and 4 metres. She wants to join them to make a new rope. The length of new rope will be .... metres.

(a) 10   (b) 9   (c) 6   (d) 7

14. Which candle is bigger than candle Q but shorter than candle P?

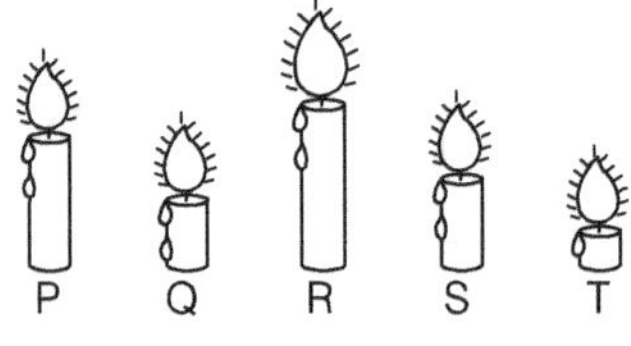

(a) T   (b) S

(c) R   (d) Both R and S

Directions (Q. Nos. 15-17) Answer the questions based on the given figure.

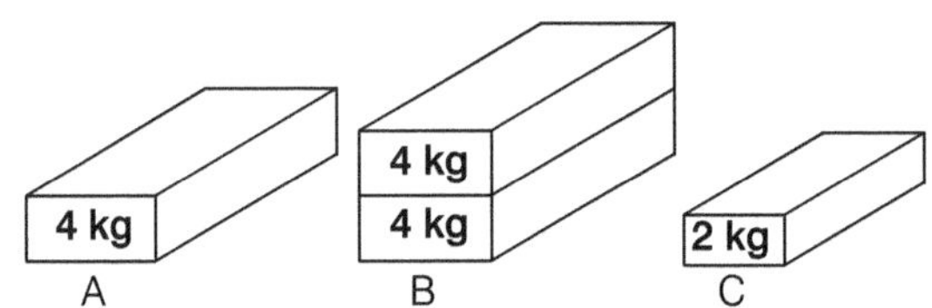

15. Which box is heaviest?

(a) A   (b) B   (c) C   (d) Can't tell

16. Which box is lightest?

(a) A   (b) B   (c) C   (d) Can't tell

17. Box B weighs .... kg more than box C.

(a) 5   (b) 6   (c) 7   (d) 8

18. The heaviest among the following is ....

(a) 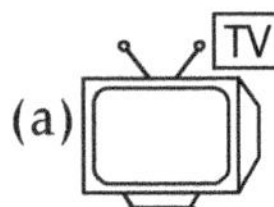

(b) 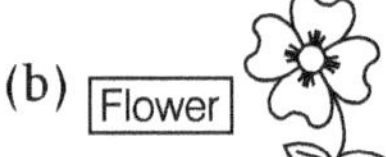

(c) 

(d) 

19. Which of the following picture shows that ball 1 is lighter than ball 2?

(a) 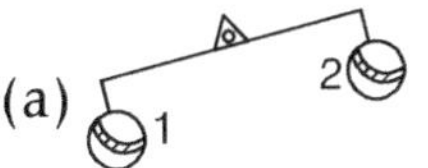   (b) 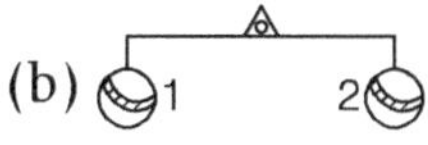   (c) 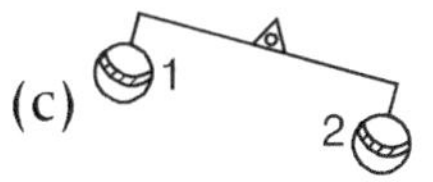   (d) None of these

20. Which of the following is heavier than the ball?

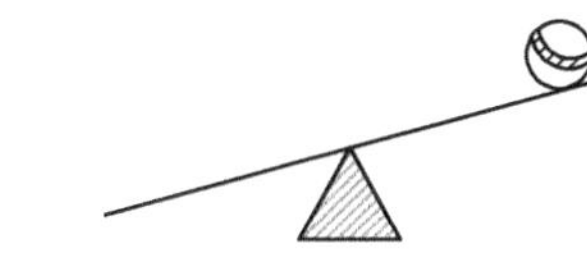

(a) 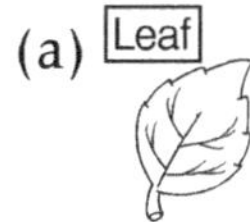   (b) 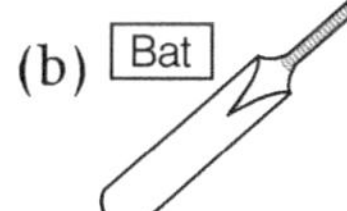   (c)    (d) 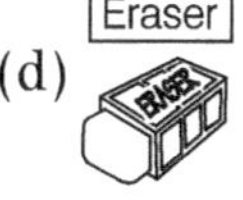

21. 3 apples weighs as much as .... mangoes.

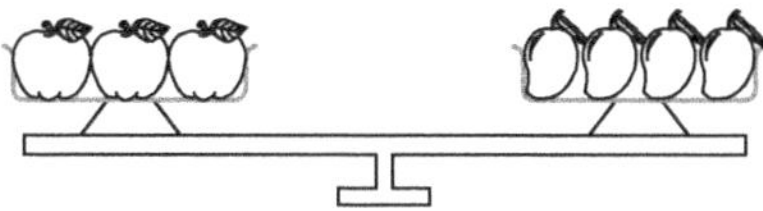

(a) 3   (b) 4   (c) 5   (d) 7

22. The heavier object is ....

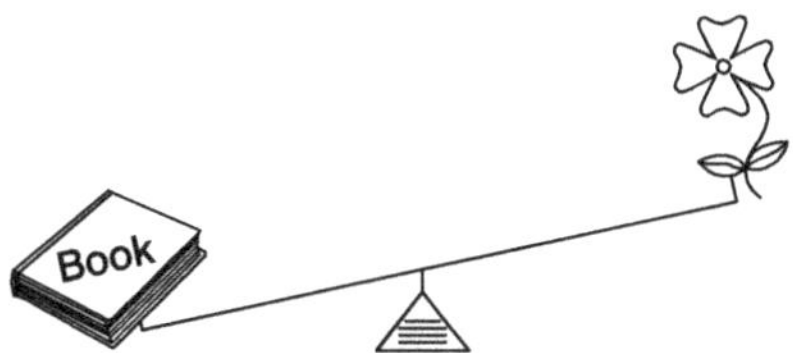

(a) Flower   (b) Book
(c) Both have same weight   (d) Can't tell

23. If each △ = 1 gram, then the weight of the box is ....

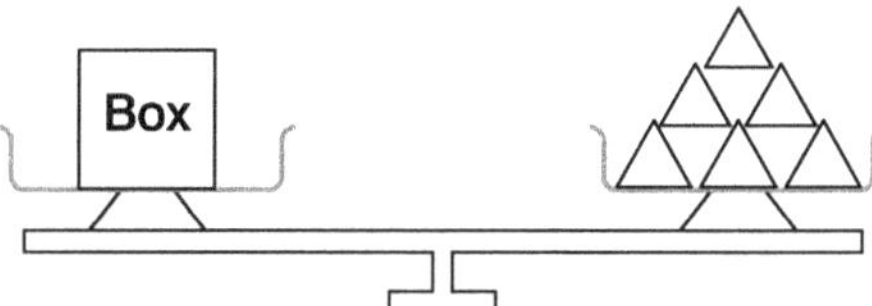

(a) 5 gm   (b) 6 gm
(c) 4 gm   (d) 12 gm

24. If weight of each  is equal to 1 unit, then the weight of book is .... units.

(a) 6   (b) 7   (c) 9   (d) 10

25. Reena weighted 20 kg when she was 10 years old. After 5 years, she weighs 40 kg. The increase in the weight of Reena is ....

(a) 10 kg   (b) 20 kg   (c) 30 kg   (d) 60 kg

26. Which bucket has the least quantity of water in it?

   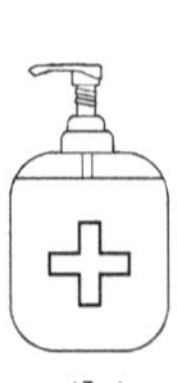      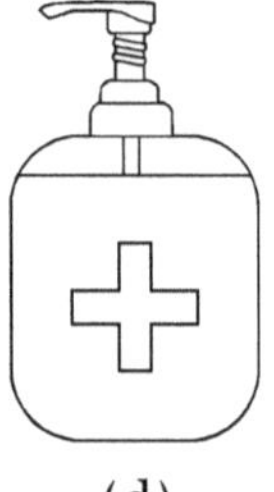

(a)   (b)   (c)   (d)

27. Which one of the following can hold more quantity sanitizer?

(a)   (b)   (c)   (d)

28. A jug can be filled by 4 glass. How much juice can the jug hold?

(a) 3 litres   (b) 4 litres

(c) 6 litres   (d) 2 litres

Money

1. The total money shown by the coins below is ....

(a) ₹ 14   (b) ₹ 15

(c) ₹ 16   (d) ₹ 17

2. Meena has      with her. Her father gave    to her.

Total money Meena has now ....

(a) ₹ 20   ₹ 10   ₹10   (b) ₹ 20   ₹ 10   ₹ 5   ₹ 2

(c) ₹ 20   ₹ 20   (d) ₹ 10   ₹ 10   ₹ 5   ₹ 5

3. Which toy has maximum cost?

(a) 

(b) 

(c) 

(d) 

22

4. Cost of ❀ is ₹ 5 .

   Then, cost of ❀❀❀❀ is ....
   - (a) ₹ 10
   - (b) ₹ 15
   - (c) ₹ 20
   - (d) ₹ 25

5. Which amount is less than ₹ 20?

   (a)
   (b)
   (c)
   (d)

6. Ankit has ₹ 10 . He bought a pack of chips worth ₹ 5 . The money left with him is
   ....
   - (a) ₹ 4
   - (b) ₹ 5
   - (c) ₹ 2
   - (d) ₹ 6

7. Rohan gave ₹ 50 to buy the toy car. How much money will he get back?

   - (a) ₹ 15
   - (b) ₹ 20
   - (c) ₹ 10
   - (d) ₹ 40

8. Purnima had ₹ 50 . She bought 3 apples for ₹ 30. How much money is
   left with her?
   - (a) ₹ 20
   - (b) ₹ 30
   - (c) ₹ 40
   - (d) ₹ 10

9. Which one of the following set of money is more than hundred rupee?

   (a)
   (c)
   (b)
   (d)

10.  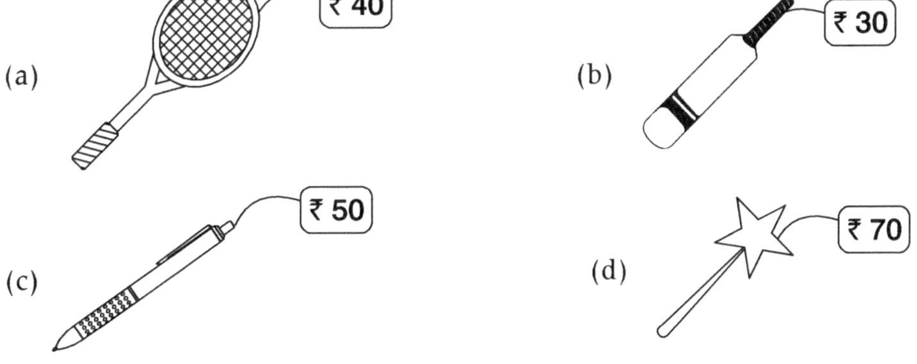 ₹ 8 [pencil] can be taken for ....

(a)  1 1

(b)  2 2

(c)  1 2 5

(d) 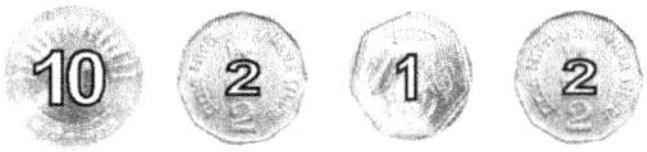 10 2 1 2

11. Sonal wants to exchange his ₹ 5 with some coins. Which set of coins can she take?

(a)  2 2 2

(b)  1 1 1

(c)  2 1 2

(d)  5 10 1

12. Neetu wants to purchase a doll for ₹ 40 .

Which of the following set of money can she use to purchase the doll?

(a)  10 10 20

(b)  5 5 5

(c)  2 5 10

(d)  10 2 1

13. One teddy bear costs ₹ 20 . How many teddy bears can be bought for ₹ 40?
(a) 2

(b) 3

(c) 4

(d) 5

14. Raghav has ₹ 50 . He pays ₹ 20 for ◯ . Now, he can purchase ....

(a) ₹ 40

(b) ₹ 30

(c) ₹ 50

(d) ₹ 70

15. Rahul has ₹ 90. Which one of the following can he buy?

(a) A doll ₹ 100

(b) A toy car ₹ 120

(c) A toy ₹ 75

(d) A pencil box for ₹ 95

Directions (Q. Nos. 16-18) Look at the price of each vegetables and answer the questions.

POTATO	TOMATO	LADYFINGER	CARROT	BRINJAL
₹ 5	₹ 4	₹ 3	₹ 2	₹ 6

16. Three carrots will cost ₹ ....

(a) 2   (b) 4   (c) 6   (d) 8

17. How much money do I pay to buy a potato?

(a) ₹ 5   (b) ₹ 4   (c) ₹ 6   (d) ₹ 3

18. How much more money do I pay to buy a brinjal than a tomato?

(a) ₹ 3

(b) ₹ 2

(c) ₹ 4

(d) ₹ 1

19. Match the item with the set of money needed to purchase it.

(A) 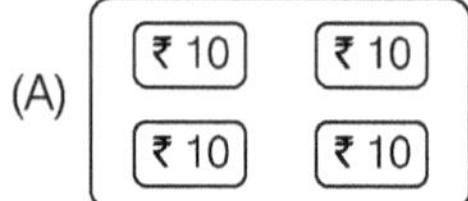

(i) 

(B) 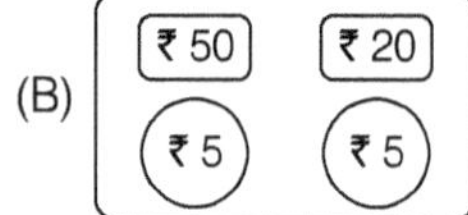

(ii) 

(C) 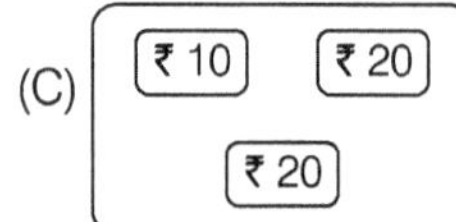

(iii) 

(D) 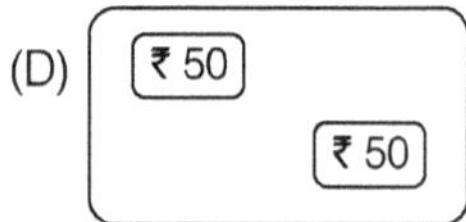

(iv) 

(a) A-ii, B-iii, C-i, D-iv

(b) A-i, B-ii, C-iii, D-iv

(c) A-iii, B-iv, C-i, D-ii

(d) A-iv, B-iii, C-ii, D-i

20. Which boy saved the less amount?

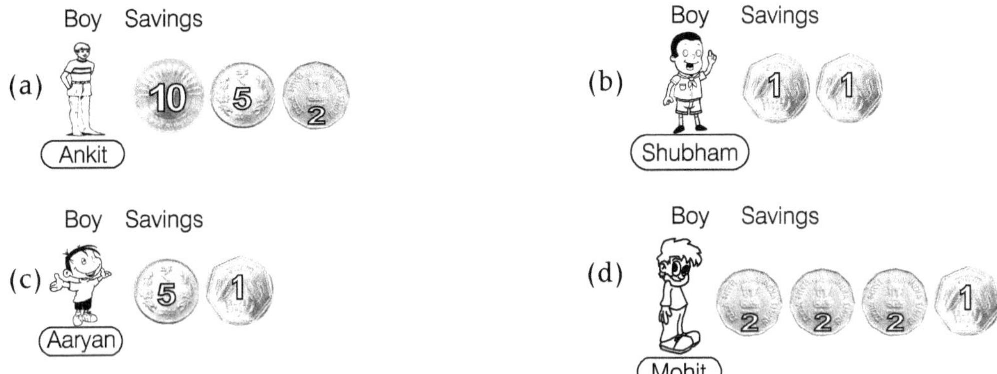

Directions (Q. Nos. 21-23) Observe the price tags and answer the questions.

LUNCH BOX	BOTTLE	SOCKS	BOOK
₹ 40	₹ 25	₹ 50	₹ 80

21. Seema has ₹ 50. How much more money does she need to buy the book?

(a) ₹ 10   (b) ₹ 30

(c) ₹ 20   (d) No need

22. Which item has the lowest amount?

(a) Lunch Box   (b) Bottle

(c) Socks   (d) Book

23. Akshay bought a lunch box and a bottle for himself. The bill paid by him was ....

(a) ₹ 90   (b) ₹ 65

(c) ₹ 85   (d) ₹ 50

Chapter 06

Time

1. Which time is called mid-night?
   (a) 11 O' clock in the night
   (b) 12 O' clock in the night
   (c) 12 O' clock in the day
   (d) 9 O' clock in the night

2. When the short hand is at 4 and the long hand is at 12, the time is ....

   (a) 3 O'clock
   (b) 4 O'clock
   (c) 5 O'clock
   (d) 6 O'clock

3. The long hand takes .... minutes to move from 2 to 3.
   (a) 1
   (b) 2
   (c) 5
   (d) 6

4. The long hand is pointing at .... minutes.

   (a) 20
   (b) 30
   (c) 35
   (d) 15

5. Which clock is showing 2 hours after 4 O'clock?

(a) 
(b) 
(c) 
(d) 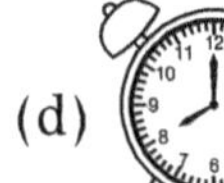
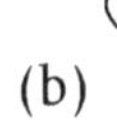

6. After 12 hours, the hour hand will be on ....

   (a) 2   (b) 12
   (c) 4   (d) 3

7. Sheela started playing at 3 : 00 pm and finished playing at 4 : 30 pm. The time taken by her is ....
   (a) 1 h 30 min   (b) 2 h
   (c) 2 h 30 min   (d) 30 min

8. Ram goes out for morning walk at 6 O'clock in the morning and comes back home after an hour. At what time does he come back?
   (a) 5 O' clock   (b) 6 O' clock
   (c) 7 O' clock   (d) 8 O' clock

9. Which activity is done at the right time?

   (a) Breakfast at 2 O'clock in the night

   (b) Sleeping at 6 O'clock in the evening

   (c) Going to school at 7 O'clock in the morning

   (d) Bathing at 5 O'clock in the evening

10. Which of the following represent 2 hour?

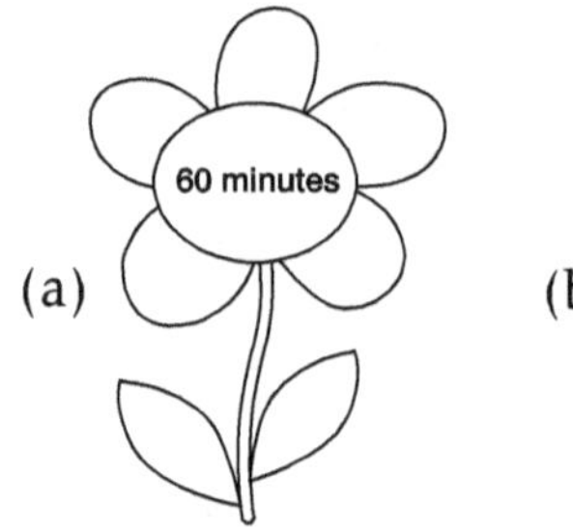

(a)

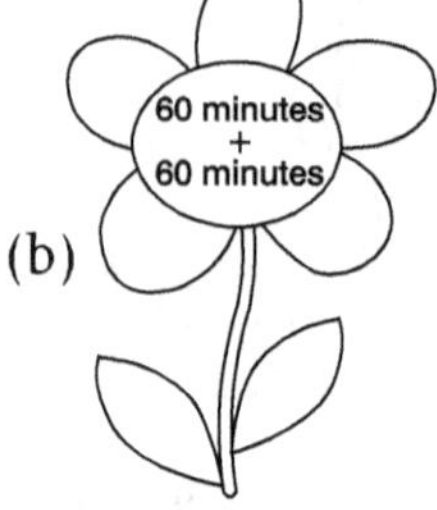

(b)

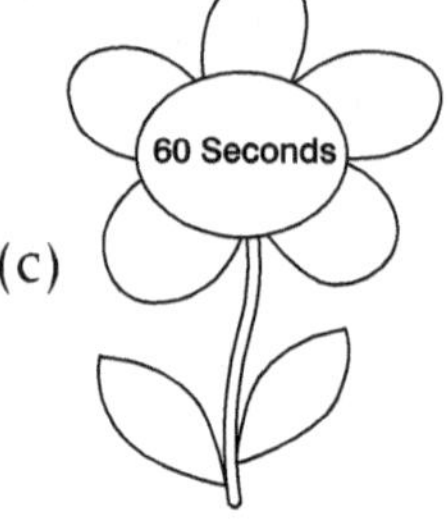

(c)

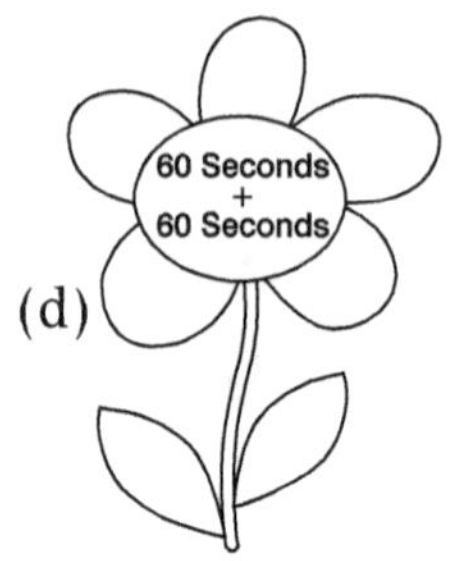

(d)

11. Study the following table to answer the given questions.

Boy	Chirag	Ishu	Shivam	Ankit
Time taken to reach the school	10 minutes	5 minutes	15 minutes	25 minutes

Who will be third to reach school?
(a) Chirag   (b) Ishu   (c) Shivam   (d) Ankit

12. How many days are there in a week?
(a) 2 days   (b) 4 days   (c) 5 days   (d) 7 days

13. Which day comes after Tuesday?
(a) Monday   (b) Wednesday
(c) Thursday   (d) Friday

14. If yesterday was Friday, then tomorrow will be ....
(a) Saturday   (b) Sunday
(c) Monday   (d) Thursday

15. How many months are there in a year?
(a) 6 months   (b) 9 months
(c) 10 months   (d) 12 months

16. How many days are in July month?
(a) 31 days   (b) 30 days
(c) 29 days   (d) 28 days

17. Which month comes just after sixth month of a year?
(a) August   (b) July
(c) June   (d) December

18. .... comes after July and before December.
(a) November   (b) March
(c) January   (d) April

Directions (Q. Nos. 19-22) Use the following calendar to answer the questions.

SUN	MON	TUE	WED	THUR	FRI	SAT
	1	2	3	4	5	6
7	8	9	10	11	12	13
14	15	16	17	18	19	20
21	22	23	24	25	26	27
28	29	30	31			

19. How many Tuesday are there in the given month?
    (a) 4   (b) 5
    (c) 6   (d) 7

20. If today is 9th of this month, then Rohan's birthday is on the 12th. How many days are left?
    (a) 2   (b) 3
    (c) 4   (d) 1

21. Third Saturday falls on which date of the given month?
    (a) 6   (b) 13
    (c) 20   (d) 27

22. The last day of the month is ....
    (a) Tuesday   (b) Wednesday
    (c) Thursday   (d) Saturday

23. Gopal's birthday is in February. On which of the following dates, his birthday cannot fall?
    (a) 27 Feb   (b) 29 Feb
    (c) 28 Feb   (d) 30 Feb

24. A leap year has .... days.
    (a) 365   (b) 366
    (c) 28   (d) 31

Shapes

1. Which of the following letter consist of straight line and curved line both?
   (a) D   (b) C   (c) T   (d) X

2. How many straight lines are there in following figure?

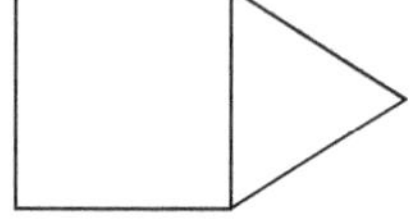

   (a) 4   (b) 5
   (c) 6   (d) 7

3. Which shape is a cylinder?

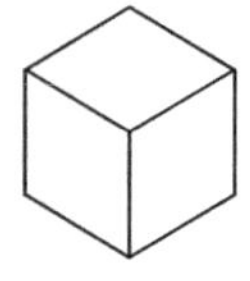

     (a)   (b)

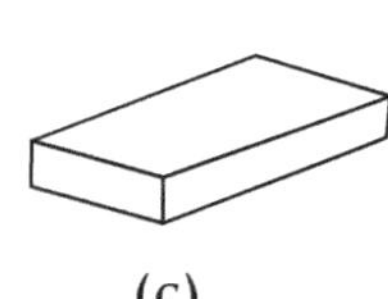

     (c)   (d)

4. Which shape is a sphere?

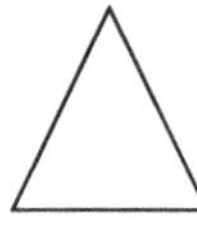

  (a)   (b)   (c)   (d)

5. What is the shape of a softy 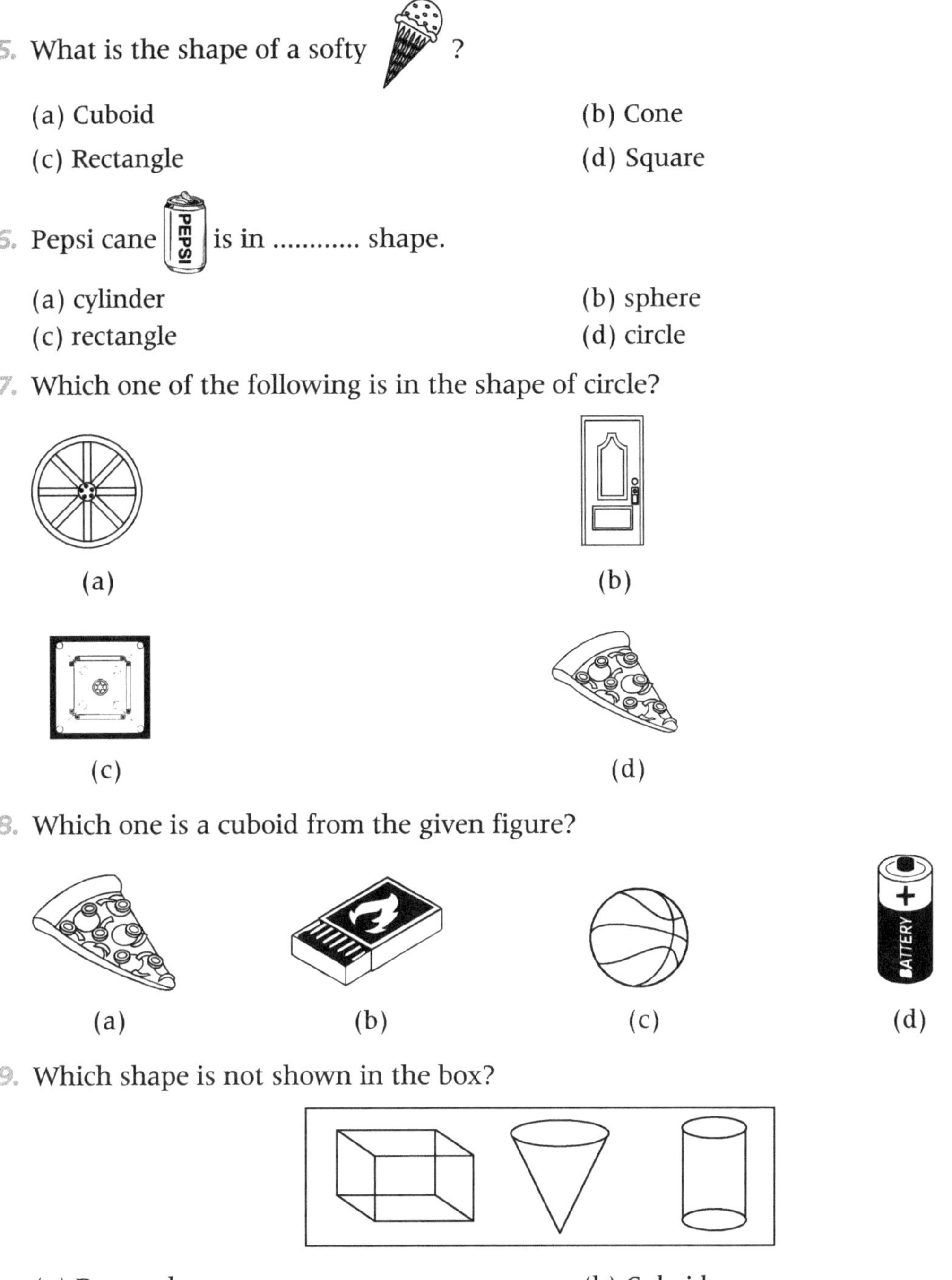 ?

   (a) Cuboid   (b) Cone

   (c) Rectangle   (d) Square

6. Pepsi cane is in .... shape.

   (a) cylinder   (b) sphere

   (c) rectangle   (d) circle

7. Which one of the following is in the shape of circle?

   (a)

   (b)

   (c)

   (d)

8. Which one is a cuboid from the given figure?

   (a)   (b)   (c)   (d)

9. Which shape is not shown in the box?

   (a) Rectangle   (b) Cuboid

   (c) Cone   (d) Cylinder

10. Name the shape of the objects kept on the table.

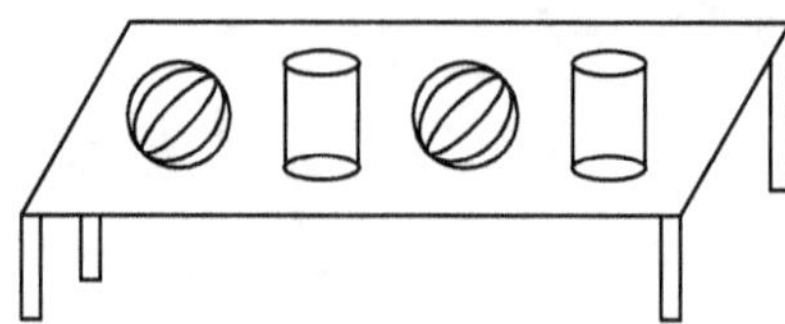

    (a) Triangle and Cylinder   (b) Cylinder and Sphere
    (c) Circle and Cone   (d) Sphere and Rectangle

11. The shape of the shaded region is a ....

    (a) triangle   (b) rectangle
    (c) circle   (d) square

12. Which shape is not shown in the given figure?

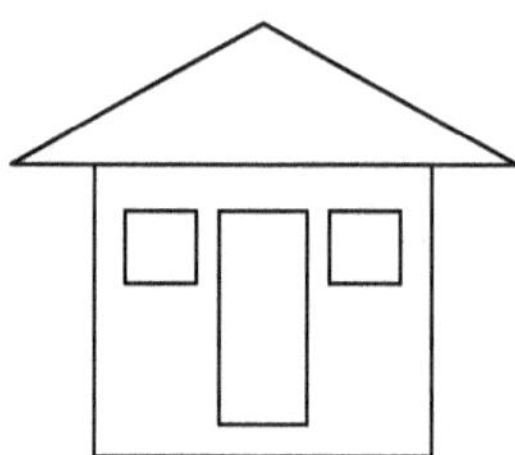

    (a) Triangle   (b) Rectangle
    (c) Circle   (d) Square

13. Which of the following is matched correctly?

(a) 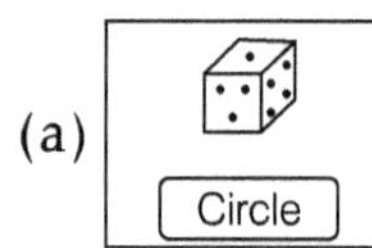

(b) 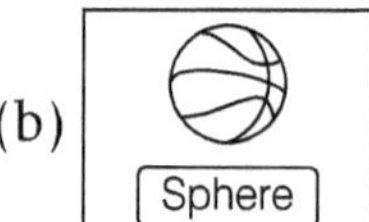

(c) 

(d) 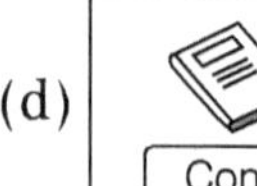

14. Match the following with their correct names and shapes.

	Column I		Column II
(A)	◯	(i)	Cuboid
(B)	△	(ii)	Rectangle
(C)	▭	(iiii)	Triangle
(D)	(cuboid figure)	(iv)	Circle

	(A)	(B)	(C)	(D)
(a)	(iii)	(iv)	(ii)	(i)
(b)	(i)	(ii)	(iv)	(iii)
(c)	(ii)	(vi)	(i)	(iii)
(d)	(iv)	(iii)	(ii)	(i)

15. A triangle has ...... sides?

(a) 3 (b) 4 (c) 1 (d) 2

16. A rectangle has ...... corner?

(a) 4 (b) 2 (c) 3 (d) 1

17. Choose the odd one out.

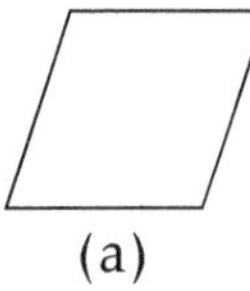  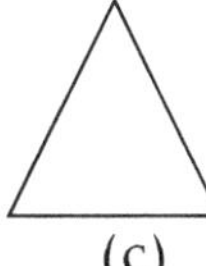 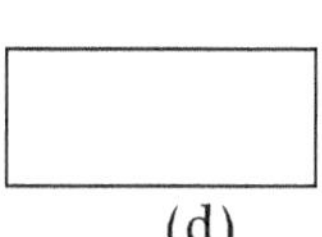

(a) (b) (c) (d)

18. Which of the following shape has 3 corners?

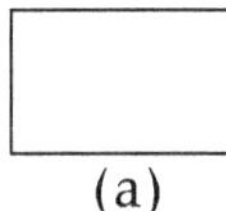 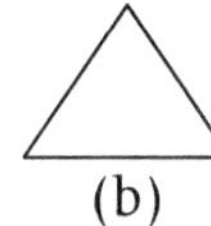  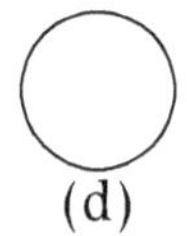

(a) (b) (c) (d)

19. Count the total number of shapes in the following figure.

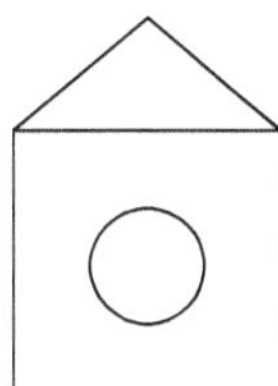

(a) 2 (b) 4 (c) 3 (d) 1

20. How many triangles are present in the box?

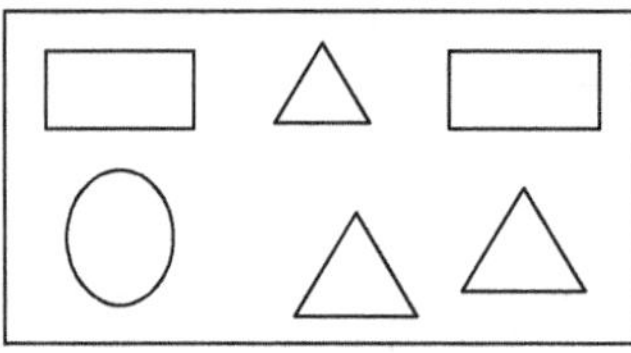

(a) 2   (b) 3

(c) 1   (d) 0

21. Count the number of rectangle and triangle shown in the given figure.

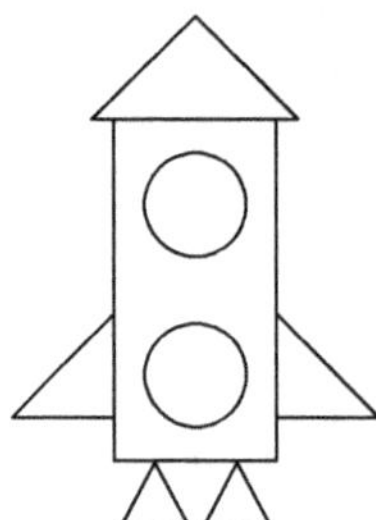

(a) 1 rectangles, 4 triangles   (b) 2 rectangles, 5 triangles

(c) 2 rectangles, 4 triangles   (d) 1 rectangle, 5 triangles

22. Shapes .... and .... will combine to form a cone.

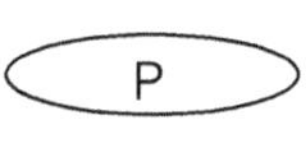 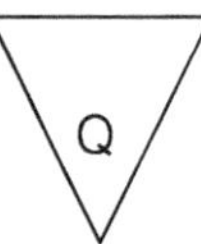  

(a) P, Q   (b) P, S

(c) R, S   (d) R, P

23. How many rectangles are present in the given figure?

(a) 17   (b) 18

(c) 16   (d) 15

Patterns

1. What comes next in the given pattern?

?

(a) 

(b) 

(c) 

(d) None of these

2. What comes next in the given pattern?

 ?

(a) 

(b) 

(c) 

(d)

3. Complete the following pattern.

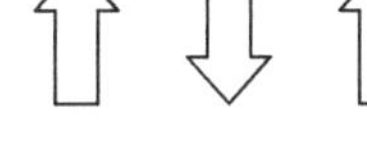

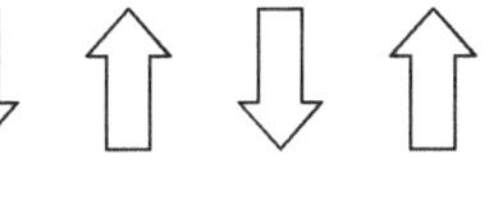

(a) 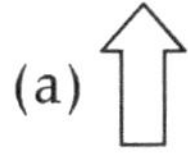

(b) 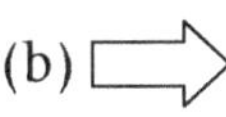

(c) 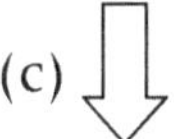

(d) None of these

4. What comes next in the given pattern?

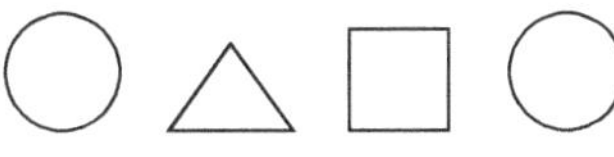

(a) 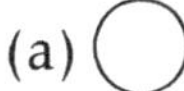

(b) 

(c) 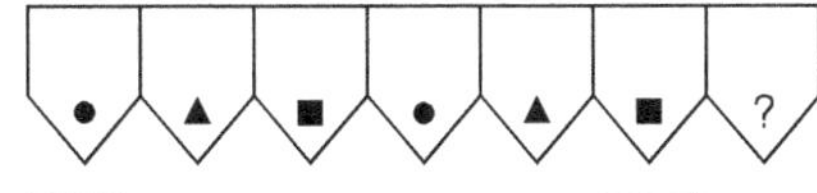

(d)

(a) 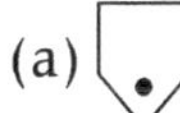

(b) 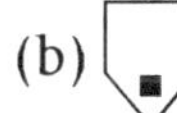

(c) 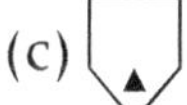

(d) 

5. Complete the pattern.

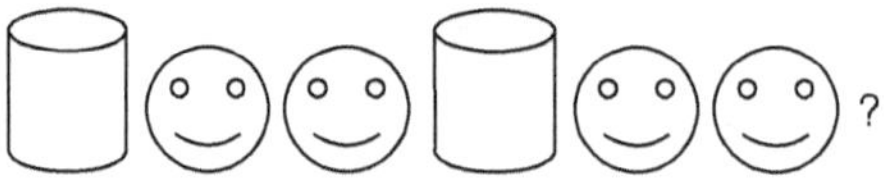

(a)    (b)    (c)    (d)

6. What will be the next to complete the following pattern?

(a)    (b)    (c)    (d)

7. What will be the next figure to complete the pattern?

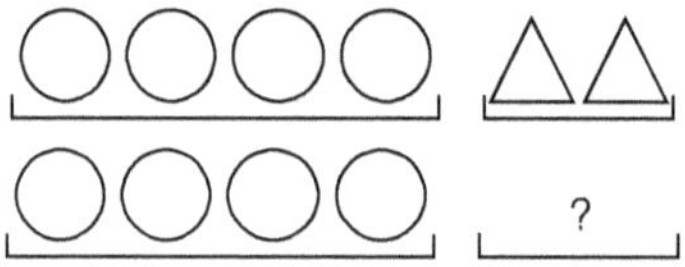

(a)   (b) 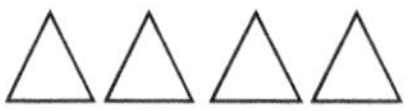   (c)    (d)

8. Which figure would come next in the pattern below.

(a)    (b)

(c)    (d) None of these

9. What will come in place of question mark?

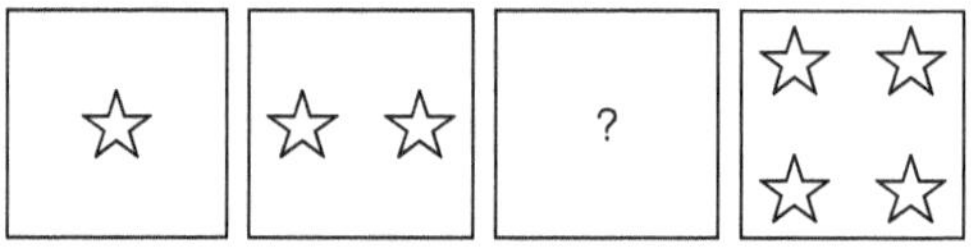

(a)    (b)    (c)    (d) None of these

10. Which figure will come next?

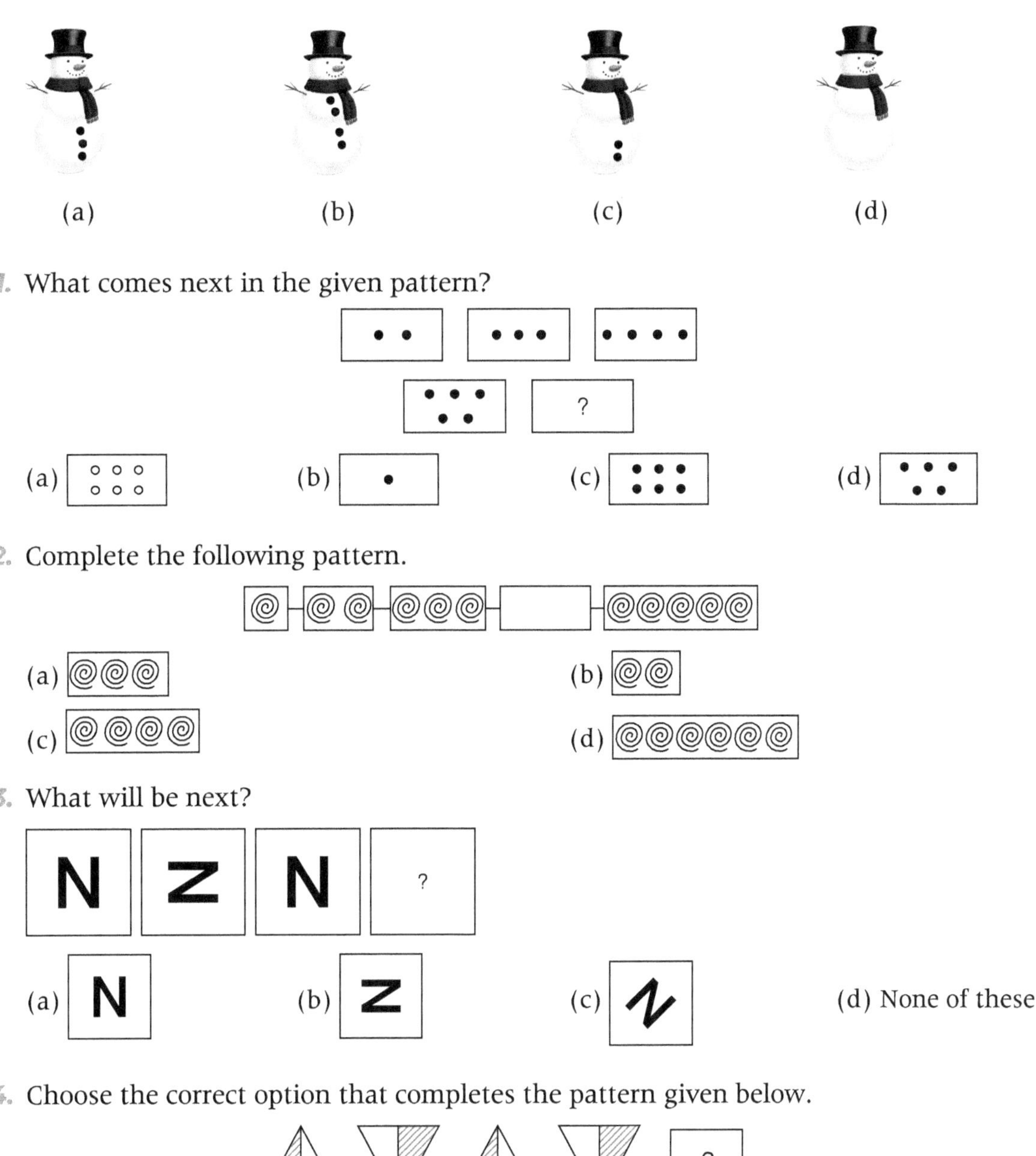

(a)   (b)   (c)   (d)

11. What comes next in the given pattern?

(a)   (b)   (c)   (d)

12. Complete the following pattern.

(a)   (b)

(c)   (d)

13. What will be next?

(a)   (b)   (c)   (d) None of these

14. Choose the correct option that completes the pattern given below.

(a)   (b)   (c)   (d)

15. Look at the following pattern.

How would you show this pattern using letters?

(a) ABAB   (b) AABB   (c) ABBB   (d) ABBA

16. Complete the following pattern

AAA   BBB   ...?...

(a) DDD   (b) CCC   (c) CC   (d) DD

17. What comes next in the following pattern?

1   12   123   1234   ...?...

(a) 12   (b) 123   (c) 125   (d) 12345

18. Study the following pattern and choose the correct option.

10   12   14   18   20

(a) 16   (b) 22   (c) 24   (d) 8

19. What will come in the blank circle?

(a) 29   (b) 31   (c) 20   (d) 5

20. Complete the pattern given below.

(a) 10   (b) 12

(c) 30   (d) 20

21. Complete the following pattern.

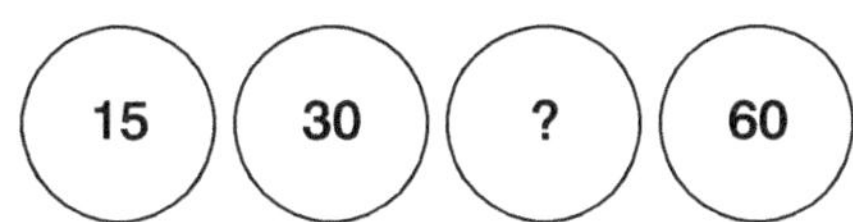

(a) 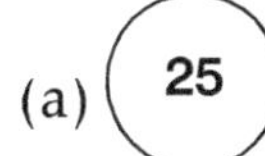 25   (b) 45   (c) 40   (d) 35

22. Study the following pattern and fill in the missing number.

1	2	3	4
2	3	4	5
?	?	?	?
4	5	6	7

(a) 5678   (b) 3254   (c) 3456   (d) 4321

23. Study the following pattern and choose correct answer.

50, 55, 60, 65, 70, 75, ...

(a) Skip counting by 5   (b) Skip counting by 2
(c) Skip counting by 3   (d) Skip counting by 4

24. Choose the correct option for the following pattern.

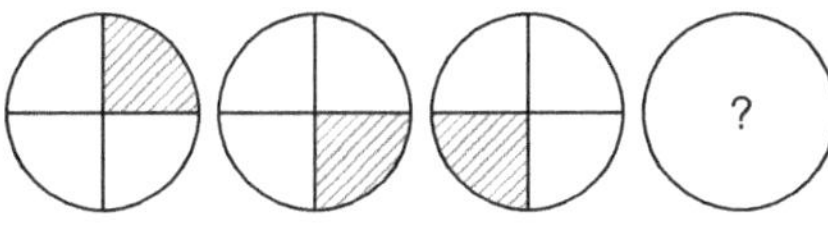

(a)    (b) 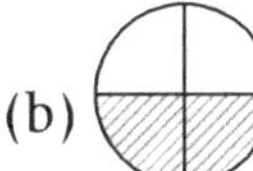   (c) 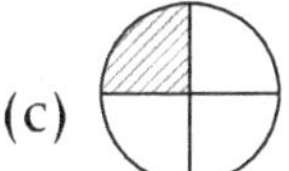   (d) None of these

25. Complete the given pattern.

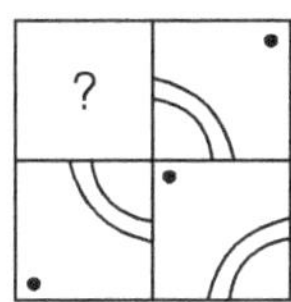

(a) 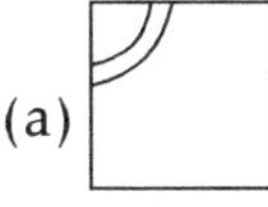   (b) 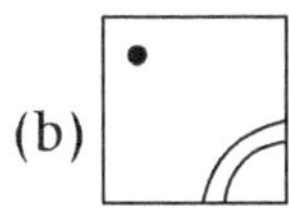

(c) 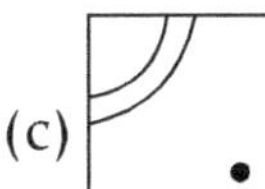   (d) 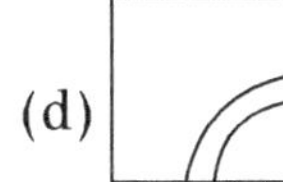

Data Handling

Directions (Q.Nos. 1-6) Look at the picture graph of different toys given below and answer the questions.

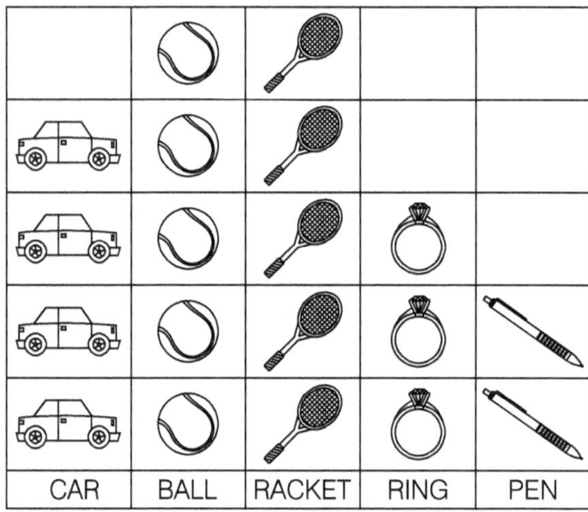

1. Which toy is least in number?
   (a) Car
   (b) Pen
   (c) Ball
   (d) Ring

2. Which two toys are same in number?
   (a) Cars and Balls
   (b) Balls and Rings
   (c) Balls and Rackets
   (d) Rings and Pens

3. How many  are there?

   (a) 3
   (b) 4
   (c) 5
   (d) 6

4. How many 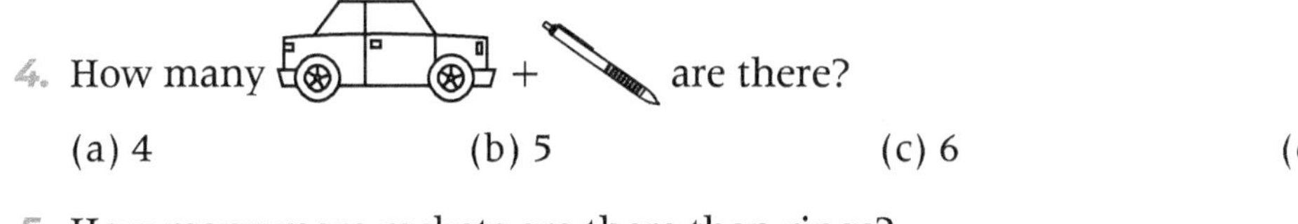 + are there?

   (a) 4   (b) 5   (c) 6   (d) 7

5. How many more rackets are there than rings?

   (a) 5   (b) 2   (c) 3   (d) 0

6. How many less cars are there than balls?

   (a) 1   (b) 0   (c) 2   (d) 3

Directions (Q. Nos. 7-9) The quantities of different vegetables grown by a farmer into his garden is shown below and now, answer the questions.

Vegetables names	Number of vegetables
Carrots	🥕🥕🥕🥕🥕🥕🥕🥕
Potatoes	🥔🥔🥔🥔🥔
Mushrooms	🍄🍄🍄🍄🍄🍄
Brinjals	🍆🍆🍆🍆

7. Difference between the number of carrots and mushrooms is ....

   (a) 1   (b) 2

   (c) 3   (d) 4

8. How many potatoes are grown into the garden?

   (a) 4   (b) 5

   (c) 6   (d) 8

9. .... types of vegetables are grown by the farmer into his garden.

   (a) 5   (b) 6

   (c) 4   (d) 3

10. Which of the two figures shows same number of pineapple?

   (a) 1 and 2   (b) 3 and 4

   (c) 2 and 4   (d) 1 and 3

Directions (Q.Nos. 11-13) Read the pictograph below and answer the following questions.

The following pictograph shows the number of books read on different days.

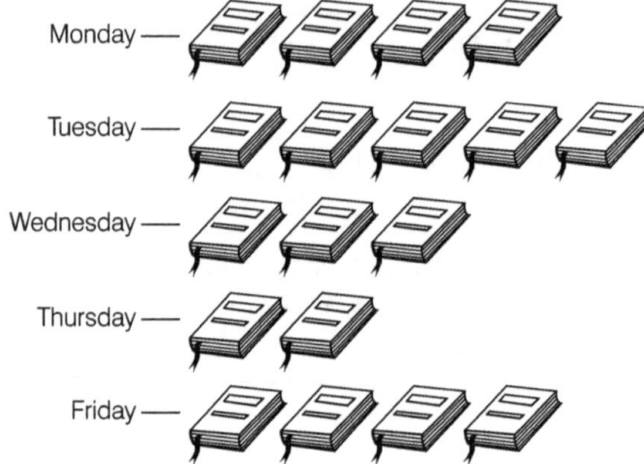

11. How many books were read on Wednesday?
(a) 10
(b) 4
(c) 3
(d) 2

12. On which day were the maximum number of books read?
(a) Monday
(b) Thursday
(c) Wednesday
(d) Tuesday

13. Two books were read in which day?
(a) Tuesday
(b) Friday
(c) Thursday
(d) Monday

Direction (Q.No. 14) Look at the picture graph given below to answer the following question.

14. How many more frogs are there than butterflies?
(a) 8
(b) 6
(c) 3
(d) 2

Directions (Q.Nos. 15 and 16) Look at the picture graph given below to answer the following questions.

It shows the number of leaves collected by 5 friends.

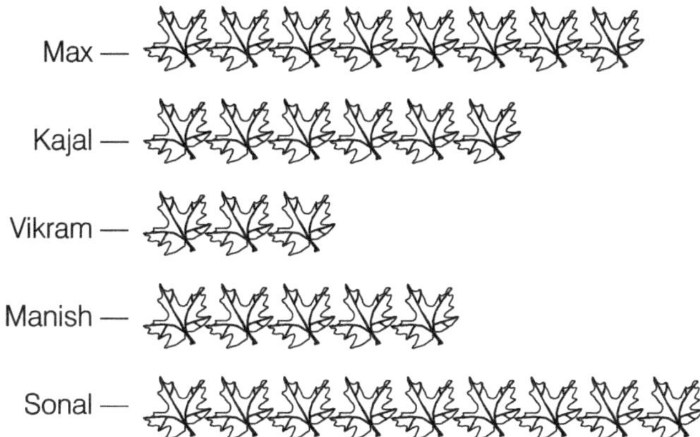

15. How many leaves did Sonal collect?
    (a) 6   (b) 10
    (c) 3   (d) 9

16. Who collected least number of leaves?
    (a) Vikram   (b) Sonal
    (c) Max   (d) Manish

Direction (Q.No. 17) Look at the picture graph given below to answer the following question.

17. Which table shows the correct number of T-shirts and Pants?

(a) 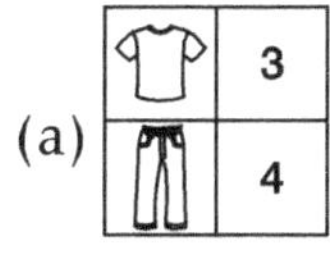

(b) 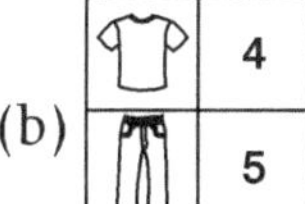

(c) 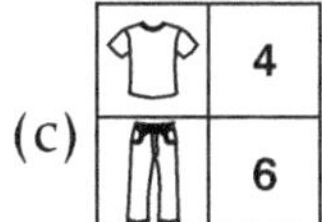

(d) 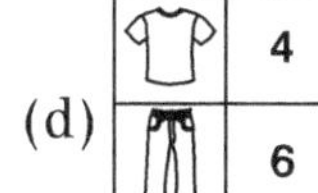

Directions (Q.Nos. 18 and 19) Observe the table carefully and answer the questions.
Rohan noted the marks of some students in Mathematics in the form of following table.

S.No.	Name of students	Marks
1.	Aprajita	80
2.	Shilpi	99
3.	Dheeraj	76
4.	Abhishek	95
5.	Ajeet	83

18. Who has scored maximum marks in Mathematics?
(a) Shilpi
(b) Dheeraj
(c) Aprajita
(d) Abhishek

19. What is the marks of Dheeraj.
(a) 99
(b) 95
(c) 83
(d) 76

Directions (Q. Nos. 20-23) The graph given below shows the number of pencils sold in a week. Study the graph and answer the questions.

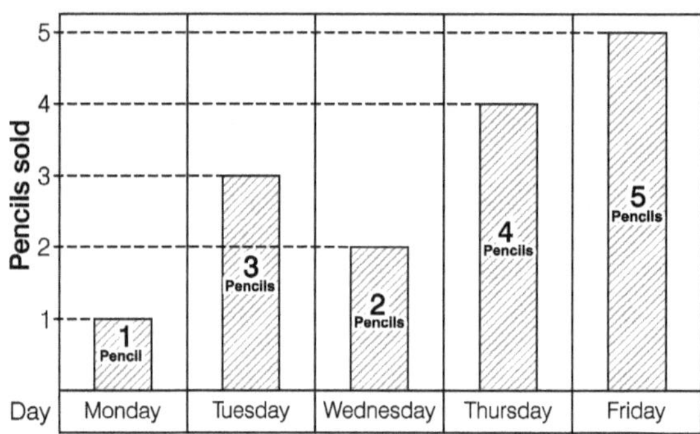

20. How many pencils were sold on Thursday?
(a) 2
(b) 4
(c) 3
(d) 5

21. On which day, the minimum number of pencils were sold?
(a) Monday
(b) Tuesday
(c) Wednesday
(d) Thursday

22. On which day, two pencils were sold?
(a) Monday
(b) Tuesday
(c) Friday
(d) Wednesday

PRACTICE SET  01

1. What shape is missing in the given pattern?

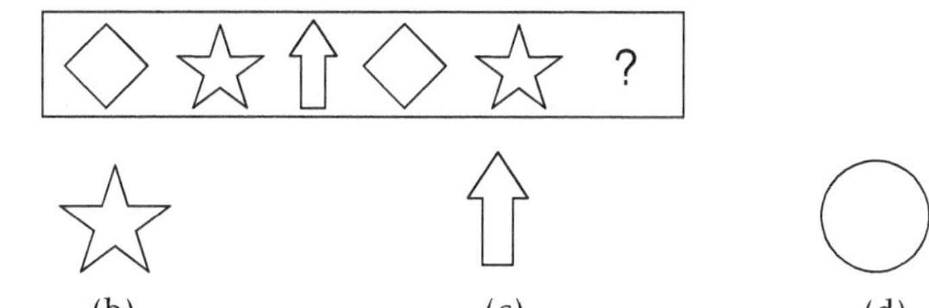

(a)   (b)   (c)   (d)

2. How many more ☆ do you need to balance the scale, if 1 ☆ = 1 ◯ ?

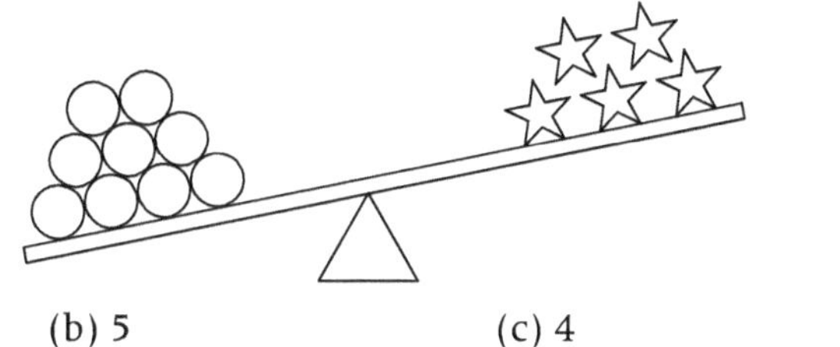

(a) 3   (b) 5   (c) 4   (d) 6

3. Number of circles in the given figure are __________ .

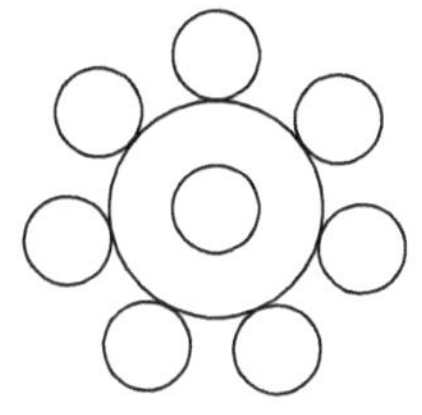

(a) 8   (b) 9   (c) 10   (d) 12

4. Fill the missing number in the given pattern.

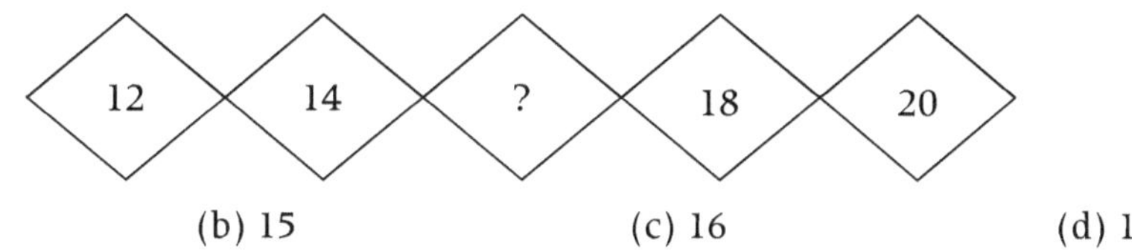

(a) 10   (b) 15   (c) 16   (d) 19

5. My mother has 12 potatoes. She uses 6 potatoes. How many potatoes are left with her?
(a) 5   (b) 7   (c) 6   (d) 8

6. Complete the given pattern. $\boxed{3\ A}$, $\boxed{5\ B}$, $\boxed{7\ C}$, $\boxed{9\ D}$, $\boxed{}$, $\boxed{13\ F}$

    (a) $\boxed{11\ H}$ (b) $\boxed{10\ E}$ (c) $\boxed{11\ D}$ (d) $\boxed{11\ E}$

7. Fill the appropriate number in the box.

2 tens	3 ones	+	5 tens	1 one	=	?	4 ones

    (a) 6 tens   (b) 8 tens   (c) 7 tens   (d) 9 tens

8. If the last month was January and the next month is March. Which month is now?
    (a) May   (b) April   (c) June   (d) February

9. Which day comes before Sunday?
    (a) Monday   (b) Tuesday   (c) Saturday   (d) Wednesday

10. If an ice-cream costs ₹ 10 and a chocolate costs ₹ 5. How much

total money Rahul needs to buy one ice-cream and two chocolates?
    (a) ₹ 15   (b) ₹ 20   (c) ₹ 28   (d) ₹ 10

11. What is the time shown in the clock?

    (a) 2 O'clock   (b) 4 O'clock   (c) 3 O'clock   (d) 5 O'clock

12. How many eight are there in the given sum?

43	+	45	=	?

    (a) 2   (b) 4   (c) 3   (d) 1

13. How many rectangles long is the pen?

1 Rectangle

    (a) 9   (b) 8   (c) 10   (d) 7

14. Which box has more lines?

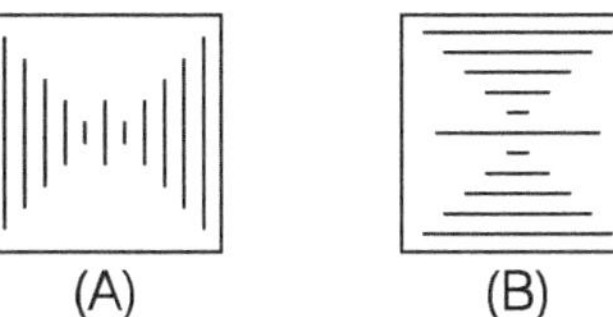

(A)   (B)

(a) A   (b) B
(c) Both have equal lines   (d) None of these

15. Which of the following two shapes make a total weight of 10 kg?

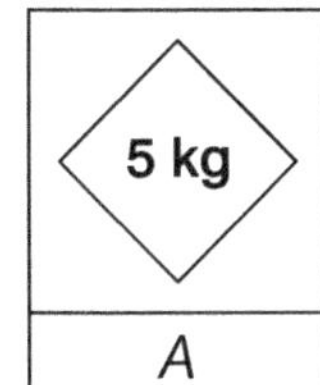 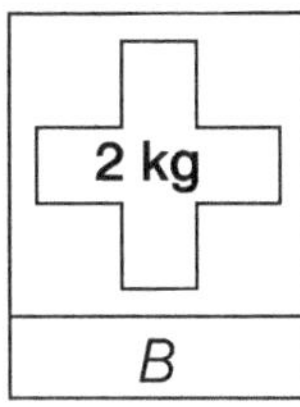 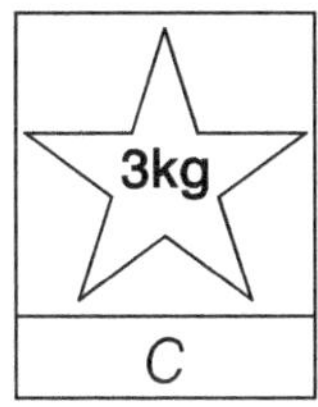 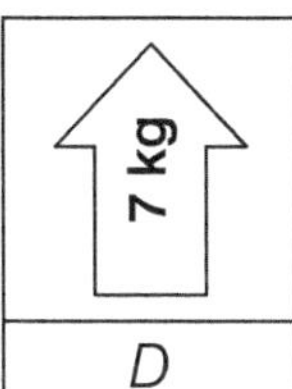

| A | B | C | D |

(a) A and D   (b) B and C   (c) C and D   (d) B and D

16. Weight of the box is ___________ .

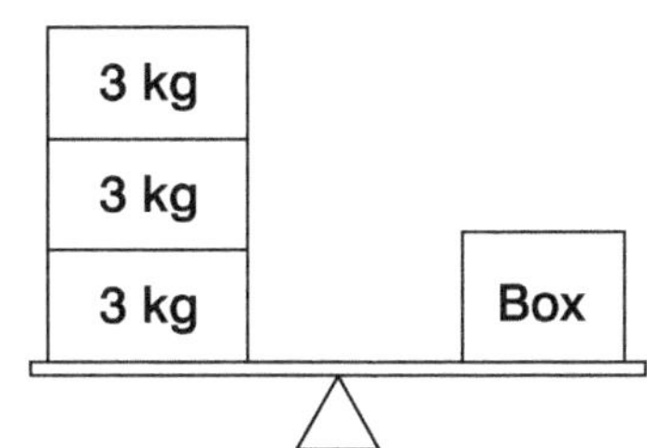

(a) 8 kg   (b) 10 kg   (c) 9 kg   (d) 11 kg

Directions (Q. Nos. 17-20) Look at the picture given below and answer the questions.

Toffee	🍬🍬🍬🍬🍬
Ice-cream	🍦🍦🍦
Balloon	🎈🎈🎈🎈
Car	🚗

17. How many more toffees are there than ice-creams?

(a) 1   (b) 3

(c) 2   (d) 4

18. Which item is four in number?

(a) Car   (b) Ice-cream

(c) Balloon   (d) Toffee

19. Total number of all the items are _________ .

(a) 12   (b) 11

(c) 14   (d) 13

20. I am more in numbers than ice-creams but less in numbers than toffees. What I am?

(a) Car   (b) Balloon

(c) Ice-cream   (d) Toffee

21. Which number will come in place of (?) ?

67   68   ?   70

(a) sixty seven   (b) sixty eight

(c) sixty nine   (d) seventy

22. Which of the following is arranged in ascending order of counting?

(a) 33   47   74   89   (b) 89   47   33   74

(a) 33   74   89   47   (c) 47   89   33   74

23. Find the sum of the smallest and the greatest number on the candies.

64   56   13   66   49

(a) 62   (b) 77

(c) 130   (d) 79

24. Which of the following amount is equal ₹ 75?

(a)

(b)

(c)

(d)

25. Pooja bought a ice-cream can as shown in the picture. The shape of the ice-cream is _____ .

(a) a sphere   (b) a cuboid   (c) a cylinder   (d) a cone

26. Which of the following options shows the correct subtraction.

(a)

(b)

(c) 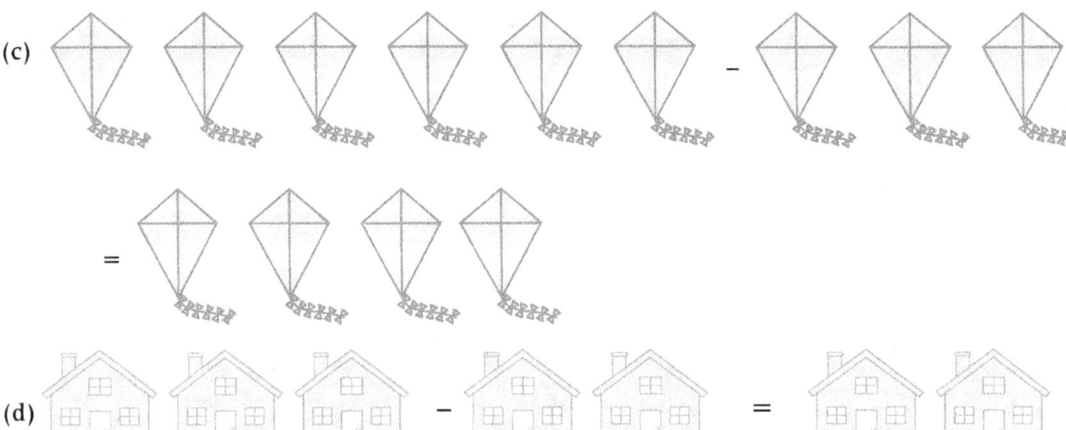

27. Study the given pictures carefully and fill in the blanks

    P : _______ tree is that tallest

    Q : ______ tree is taller than tree *A* but shorter than *E*.

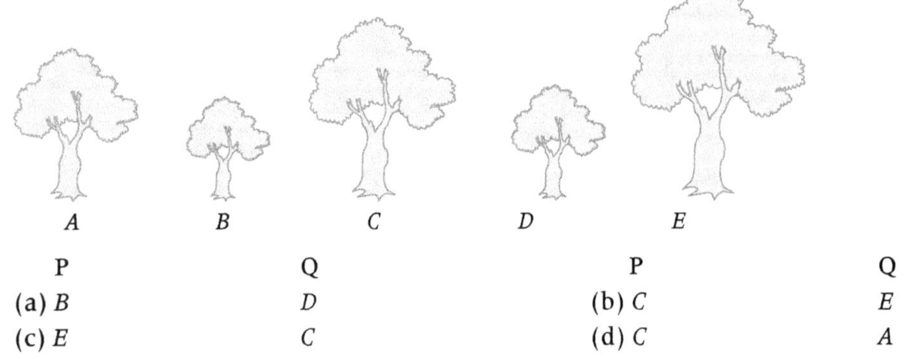

	P	Q		P	Q
(a)	*B*	*D*	(b)	*C*	*E*
(c)	*E*	*C*	(d)	*C*	*A*

28. In a yr September has ______ days.

    (a) 30   (b) 29   (c) 31   (d) 28

29. Which shape is not present in the given cloud.

    (a) Circle

    (b) Cylinder

    (c) Cone

    (d) Rectangle

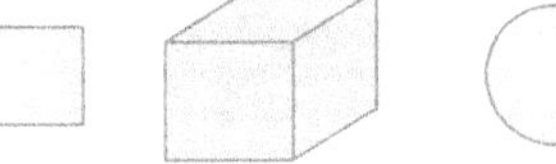

30. Julee has 37 doll toys. Her sister gave her 11 doll toys. How many doll toys does she have now?

(a) 26   (b) 47   (c) 48   (d) 36

31. Rajni had

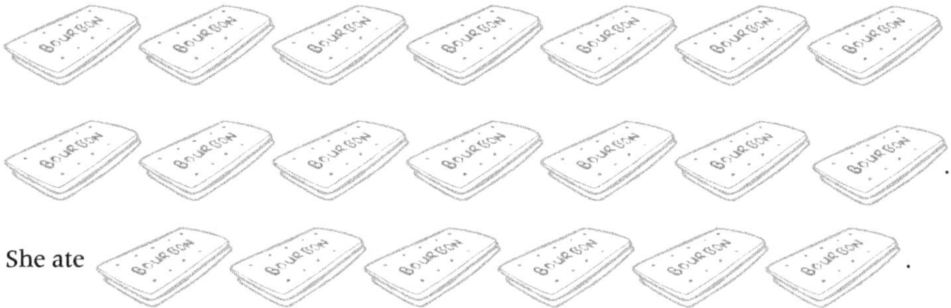

She ate 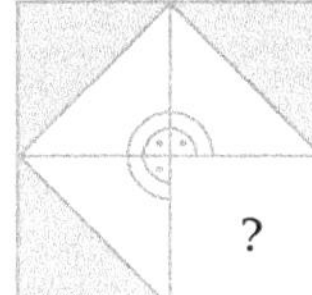 

How many Biscuit fig are left with her.

(a) 6   (b) 8
(c) 7   (d) 9

32. Which of the following options will complete the pattern in the given figure?

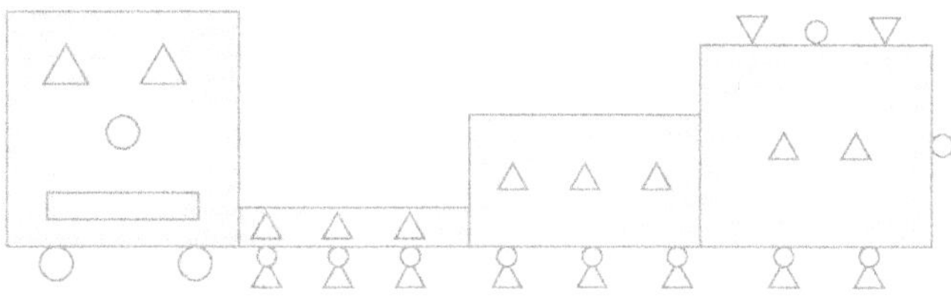

(a)   (b)   (c)   (d)

33. Total number of triangles in the following toy figure is ______ .

(a) 18   (b) 19   (c) 20   (d) 22

34. Select the odd one out.

(a)　　　　　(b)　　　　　(c)　　　　　(d)

35. Study the given pictures carefully and match the following.

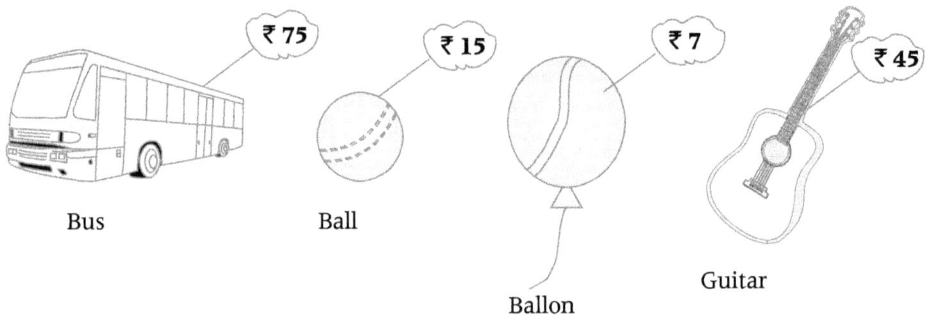

	Column I		Column II
X	Total cost of a ball and a guitar is ______ .	1.	₹ 30
Y	Cost of a bus is ______ more than the cost of a guitar.	2.	₹ 8
Z	Cost of a ballon is ______ less than the cost of a ball.	3.	₹ 60

	X	Y	Z			X	Y	Z
(a)	1	2	3		(b)	3	1	2
(c)	2	3	1		(d)	1	3	2

PRACTICE SET 02

1. Mark the time shown by the clock.

   (a) 11 O'clock   (b) 12 O'clock   (c) 10 O'clock   (d) 4 O'clock

2. Raghav has 6 toy cars. He gave 2 toy cars to his sister. How many toy cars are left with him?

   (a) 3   (b) 5   (c) 4   (d) 6

3. Choose the option having numbers arranged in ascending order.

   (a) 24, 36, 15, 20, 11   (b) 15, 16, 20, 19, 35

   (c) 11, 14, 22, 35, 46   (d) 45, 11, 15, 6, 17

4. Starting with Monday, which is the fourth day of the week?

   (a) Wednesday   (b) Thursday

   (c) Tuesday   (d) Friday

5. Fill the box with correct number.

   | 7 tens 4 ones | − | 4 tens 2 ones | = | 3 tens ? ones |

   (a) 1   (b) 3   (c) 2   (d) 4

6. Add the money and choose the correct option.

   (a) ₹ 25   (b) ₹ 15

   (c) ₹ 20   (d) ₹ 5

7. Fill the missing numbers counting by 2.

44	46	?	50	52	?	?

(a) 47, 53, 54 (b) 48, 54, 56 (c) 47, 54, 56 (d) 48, 50, 54

8. Which one of the following numbers is more than $6+5$?

(a) 12 (b) 8 (c) 9 (d) 10

9. How many squares are there in the given figure?

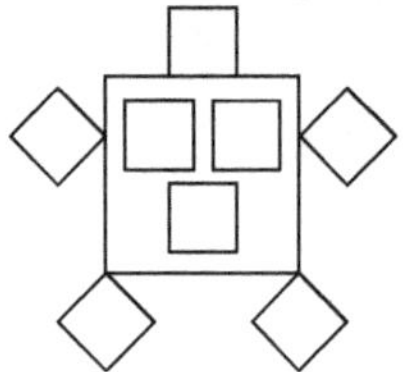

(a) 9 (b) 8 (c) 7 (d) 10

10. Which one of the following coin has the highest value?

(a)  (b)  (c)  (d) 

11. Which of the following is in triangular shape?

(a)  (b) 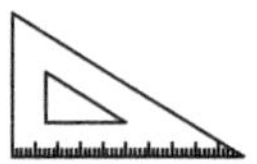 (c)  (d) 

12. Choose the correct sum from the abacus given below.

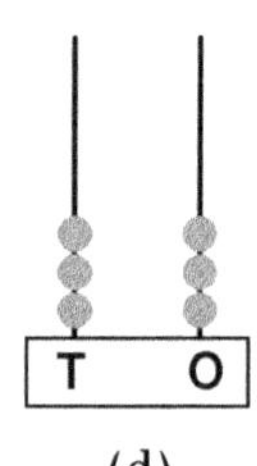

13. If Sunday is the first day of the week, then name the last day of the week?

(a) Monday   (b) Tuesday   (c) Wednesday   (d) Saturday

14. Smith is reading a book. He is on page number 20. The next page number will be

__________ .

(a) 23   (b) 19   (c) 21   (d) 22

15. In a class of 28 children, there are 12 boys. How many girls are there in the class?

(a) 14   (b) 15   (c) 16   (d) 17

16. Match the following.

Column I		Column II
A. 17 − 15	(i)	15
B. 9 + 4	(ii)	2
C. 15 − 0	(iii)	11
D. 8 + 3	(iv)	13

	A	B	C	D
(a)	(ii)	(iv)	(i)	(iii)
(b)	(i)	(ii)	(iii)	(iv)
(c)	(i)	(iv)	(i)	(ii)
(d)	(i)	(ii)	(iii)	(i)

17. Which of the following shape is not present in the given figure?

(a) Cylinder   (b) Circle   (c) Rectangle   (d) Triangle

18. Which of the following option shows the least value?

(a)   (b)   (c)   (d)

19. Complete the pattern given below.

$ $ ★★★ $ $ ★★★ ?

(a) ★★   (b) ★ $ (c) $ $ (d) $ ★

20. Joy has ₹ 70 , then which one of the following can he buy?

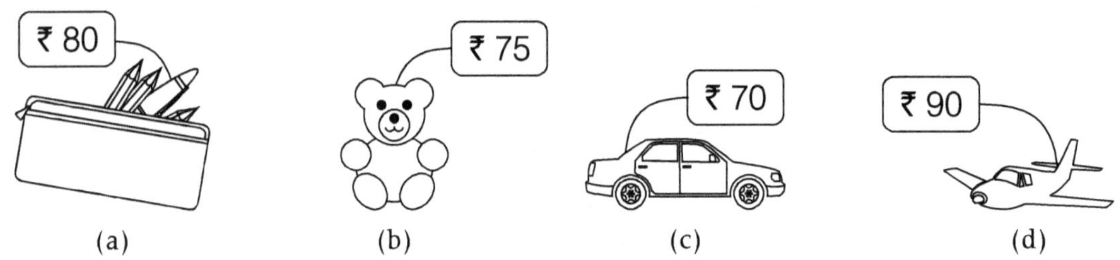

(a)   (b)   (c)   (d)

21. _______ is 4th from the left end.

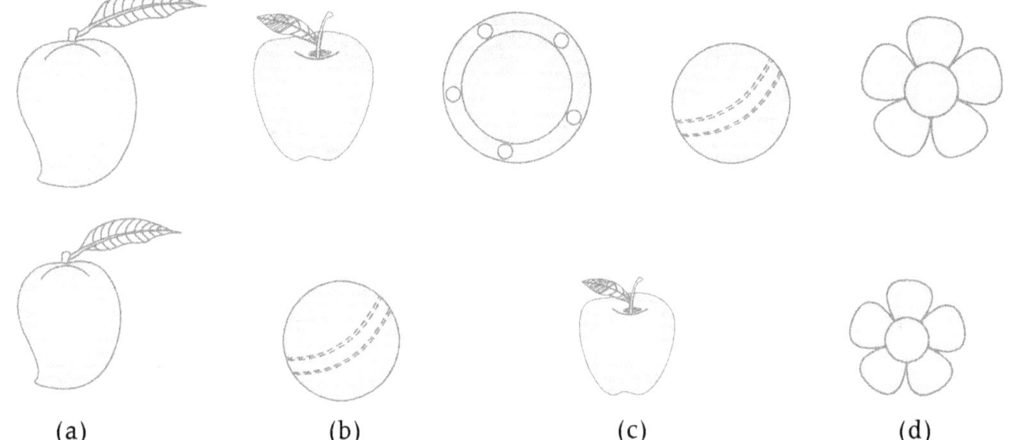

(a)   (b)   (c)   (d)

22. How many balls should be crossed (X) to show 6 ice-creams uncrossed?

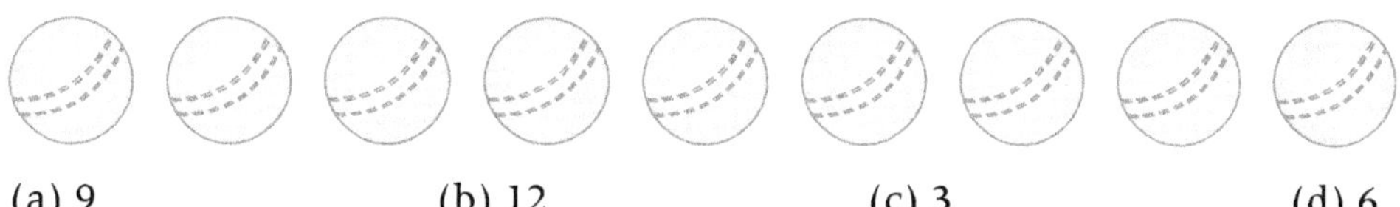

(a) 9   (b) 12   (c) 3   (d) 6

23. How many flowers are there altogether.

(a) 1 tens 8 ones   (b) 1 tens 7 ones   (c) 1 tens 6 ones   (d) 18 ones

24. Which of the following is the heaviest?

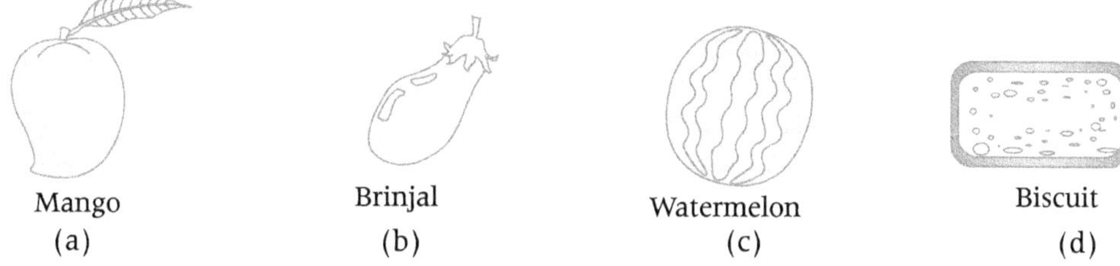

Mango   Brinjal   Watermelon   Biscuit
(a)   (b)   (c)   (d)

25. Which activity is correct?

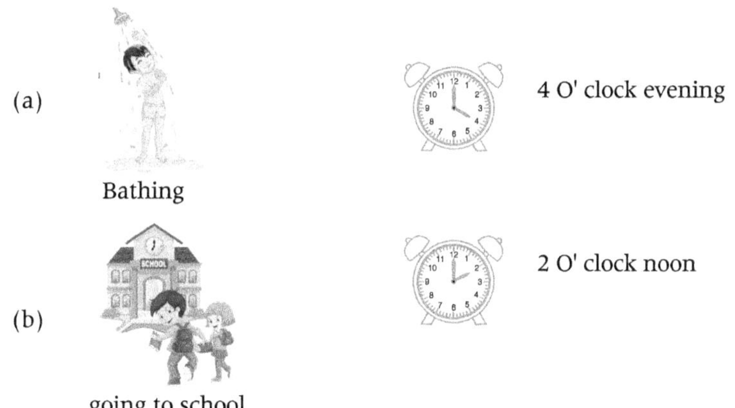

(a)

Bathing

4 O' clock evening

(b)

going to school

2 O' clock noon

(c) 
playing

 10 O' clock morning

(d) 
Lunch

 1 O' clock noon

26. If Pragya starts her coaching class on 2nd Monday of July 20XY, then on which date does she start her coaching class?

July 20XY						
Sun	Mon	Tue	Wed	Thu	Fri	Sat
				1	2	3
4	5	6	7	8	9	10
11	12	13	14	15	16	17
18	19	20	21	22	23	24
25	26	27	28	29	30	31

(a) 5th July   (b) 12th July   (c) 19th July   (d) 13th July

27. Arrange the given trees from the tallest to the shortest.

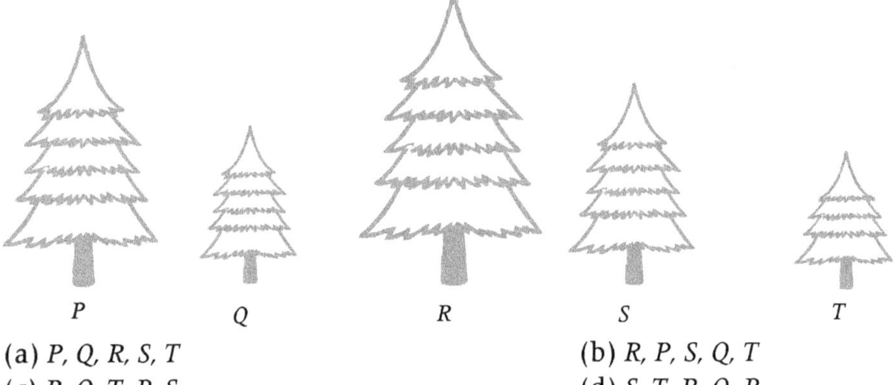

(a) *P, Q, R, S, T*   (b) *R, P, S, Q, T*

(c) *R, Q, T, P, S*   (d) *S, T, R, Q, P*

28. Piyush bought 12 kites on Monday, 10 kites on Tuesday and 17 kites on Wednesday. How many kites did he buy altogether?

(a) 39   (b) 22   (c) 27   (d) 29

29. Seema bought a cold drink can as shown in the picture. The shape of the can is ______ .

   (a) Sphere   (b) Cone   (c) Cube   (d) Cylinder

Directions (Q. Nos. 30 and 31) Look at the picture given below and answer the following questions

30. How many tigers are there in the picture?

   (a) 4   (b) 5
   (c) 6   (d) 3

31. How many (elephant) are more than)?

   (a) 1   (b) 2
   (c) 3   (d) 0

32. How many months are there in a year?
   (a) 6 months   (b) 8 months
   (c) 12 months   (d) 14 months

33. If ⬜5 ⬜ is related to ⬜ ⬜6 in same way, then in the same way ⬜7⬜ is related to _____ .

(a)   (b)   (c)   (d)

34. If yesterday was 12th date, then tomorrows will be-date of a month of the year will be.
(a) 14th   (b) 13th
(c) 11th   (d) None of these

35. The given number line shows _____ .

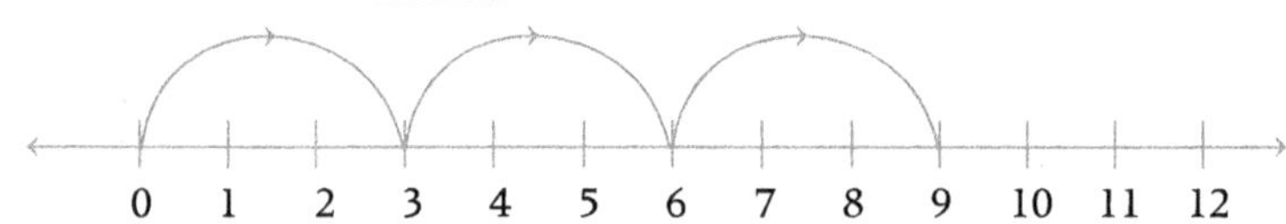

(a) Counting by 1's   (b) Counting by 2's
(c) Counting by 3's   (d) Counting by 4's

Hints & Solutions

1. Numbers 1 to 100

1. *(d)* We count the figures and write

Option	(a)	(b)	(c)	(d)
Number of figures	6 mobiles	6 pencils	6 girls	5 pieces

2. *(b)* We count the figures

Name of box	A	B	C	D
Number of figures in box	6	4	5	3

3. *(b)* We count the letters in given words.
SHAPES → 6 letters, CALENDAR → 8 letters
MONEY → 5 letters, CIRCLES → 7 letters

4. *(a)* In the given figure,
flowers pots → 4, Apples → 3
i.e there are 4 flowers pots and 3 apples.

5. *(b)* We are counting the figures,

Option	Fig. I	Fig. II
(a)	8 dots	9 dots
(b)	11 dots	11 dots
(c)	5 dots	7 dots
(d)	7 dots	5 dots

So, there are in option (b), equal dots.

6. *(a)* We are counting the number of objects in baskets

Option	Basket I	Basket II
(a)	2 objects	2 objects
(b)	2 objects	1 objects
(c)	3 objects	4 objects
(d)	5 objects	7 objects

So, there are in option (a) both baskets have equal objects.

7. *(b)* We count the figures and match.

Option	Column I	Match Column I
(A)	4	(iii) → 4
(B)	5	(iv) → 5
(C)	3	(i) → 3
(D)	8	(ii) → 8

Hence, option (b) is correct answer.

8. *(b)* According to the order of counting.

34   35   **36**   37   38

∴ ? = 36

9. *(a)* According to the order of counting

72   73   **74**   75   **76**   77

10. *(a)* We read the counting and write

Eighty one   Eighty two   Eighty tree

11. *(a)* Write the counting

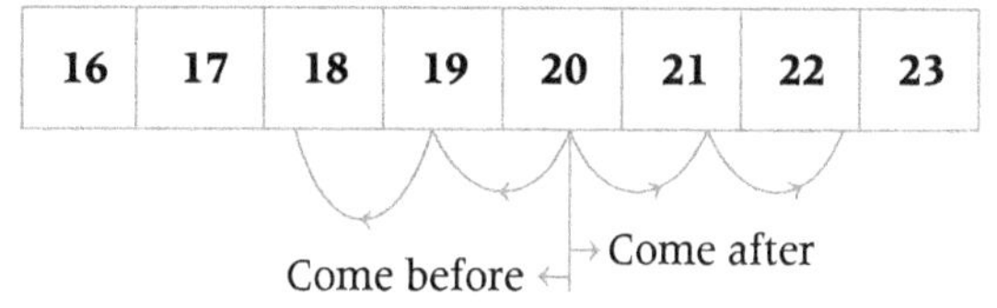

∴ 69 comes just before 70.

12. *(b)* Write the counting

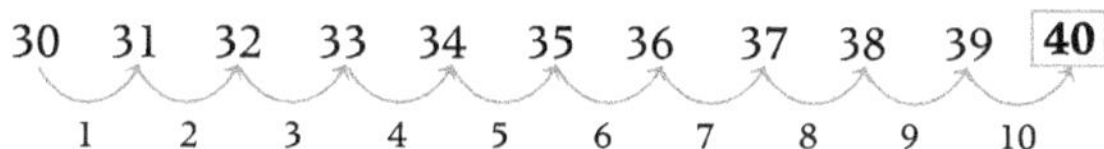

∴ 18 comes just before 20, when counting by 2.

13. *(c)* We are counting by 10 after 30, then we get

30 31 32 33 34 35 36 37 38 39 **40**
1   2   3   4   5   6   7   8   9   10

14. *(b)* In the given figure

Number of O is 5 and number of Δ is 3.

We write the counting.

Since, 3 is less than 5.

Therefore, number of Δ is less than number of O.

15. *(a)* In given abacus

$\boxed{4}$ tens and $\boxed{3}$ ones

∴ Number of tens is 4.

16. *(b)* $\boxed{59}$ = $\boxed{5}$ tens + $\boxed{9}$ ones

∴ ? = 5

17. *(a)* The place of 8 in the number 78 is ones.

18. *(b)* The place value of 2 in 72 is two ones.

19. *(c)* Given abacus,

Option (a) $\boxed{5}$ Tens and $\boxed{7}$ ones = 57

Option (b) $\boxed{6}$ Tens and $\boxed{6}$ ones = 66

Option (c) $\boxed{6}$ Tens and $\boxed{4}$ ones = 64

Option (d) $\boxed{4}$ Tens and $\boxed{6}$ ones = 46

20. *(b)* In given abacus

Option (a) $\boxed{2}$ Tens + $\boxed{5}$ ones = 25

Option (b) $\boxed{2}$ Tens + $\boxed{1}$ ones = 21

Come just after 20

Option (c) $\boxed{2}$ Tens + $\boxed{3}$ ones = 23

Option (d) $\boxed{2}$ Tens + $\boxed{0}$ ones = 20

21. *(a)* In given abacus;

Option (a) $\boxed{1}$ Tens + $\boxed{9}$ ones = 19

Come just before 20

Option (b) $\boxed{2}$ Tens + $\boxed{2}$ ones = 22

Option (c) $\boxed{2}$ Tens + $\boxed{1}$ ones = 21

Option (d) $\boxed{1}$ Tens + $\boxed{2}$ ones = 12

22. *(b)* There is 6 an even number.

23. *(a)* By counting, the number of parrots = 7 It is an odd number.

24. *(c)* Arranging the given number in order of counting

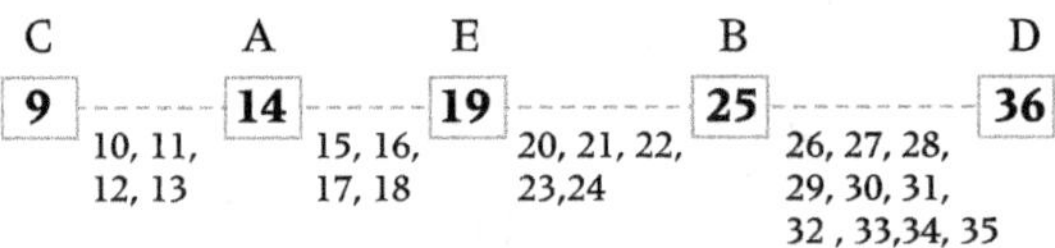

So, 36 or block D number is the highest number.

25. *(d)* Arranging the given number in order of counting

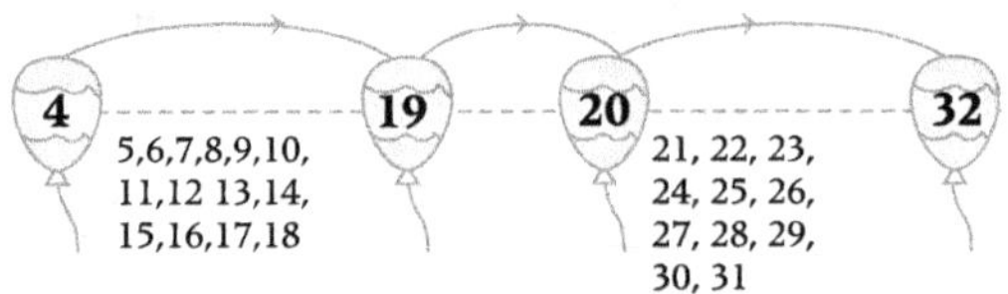

So, 4 is the smallest number

26. *(c)* Arranging the given numbers in order of counting.

Hence, option (c) is correct answer.

2. Addition

1. *(b)* Number of blue balls = 5

Number of black balls = 3

Total number of balls = 8

678

2. *(b)*

Mangoes in basket = 6

Rohan puts = 3

Total mangoes = 9

789

3. *(b)*

1   2   4   5

3   +   6   7   = 8 leaves

8   (Total leaves)

4. *(b)*

$$\begin{array}{r} 3 \\ +\quad 5 \\ \hline 8 \end{array}$$

5. *(a)* Option (a)   option (b)

$$\begin{array}{r} 6 \\ +\quad 2 \\ \hline 8 \end{array}\text{ (Correct)} \qquad \begin{array}{r} 7 \\ +\quad 0 \\ \hline 7 \end{array}\text{ (not correct)}$$

option (c)   option (d)

$$\begin{array}{r} 5 \\ +\quad 3 \\ \hline 8 \end{array}\text{ (not correct)} \qquad \begin{array}{r} 4 \\ +\quad 4 \\ \hline 8 \end{array}\text{ (not correct)}$$

6. *(a)*

$$\begin{array}{r} 5 \\ +\quad 3 \\ \hline 8 \end{array}$$

7. *(b)*

Students in class I A = 12
Students in class I B = 7
$$\overline{\text{Total number of students = 19}}$$

8. *(b)* Option (a)   option (b)

$$\begin{array}{r} 5 \\ +\quad 6 \\ \hline 11 \end{array}\text{ (not correct)} \qquad \begin{array}{r} 8 \\ +\quad 4 \\ \hline 12 \end{array}\text{ (Correct)}$$

option (c)   option (d)

$$\begin{array}{r} 1 \\ +\quad 8 \\ \hline 9 \end{array}\text{ (not correct)} \qquad \begin{array}{r} 6 \\ +\quad 4 \\ \hline 10 \end{array}\text{ (not correct)}$$

9. *(b)*

= 12
(Total ballons)

10. *(b)* Count and write the number of figures, according to the question.

5 cups + 4 rings + 6 spoons

or 5 + 4 + 6

11. *(b)*

Shirts bought on Monday = 5
Shirts bought on Tuesday = 4
Shirts bought on Wednesday = 7
$$\overline{\text{Total shirts = 16}}$$

12. *(b)* In the given pattern,

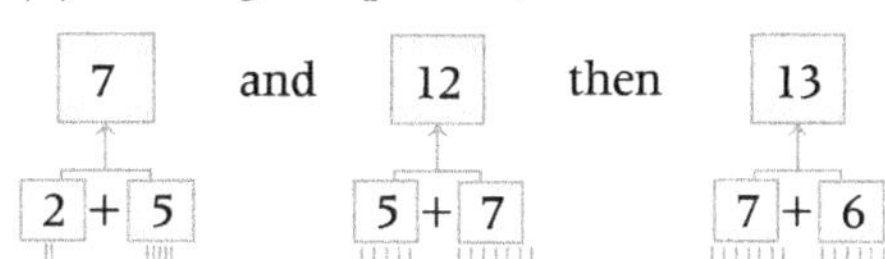

7   and   12   then   13

2 + 5   5 + 7   7 + 6

13. *(b)*

3, 2, 1 + 4, 5, 2 + 3, 1, 2

or 6 + 11 + 6 = 23

14. *(b)* In the given question,

5 figures + 6 figures

= 11 figures or 5 + 6 = 11

So, option (b) is correct relations.

15. *(a)*

$$\boxed{\begin{array}{cccc}①&②&③&④\\⑤&⑥&⑦&⑧\end{array}} + \boxed{\begin{array}{cccc}⑨&⑩&⑪&⑫\\⑬&⑭&⑮&\end{array}} = \boxed{15}$$

So, there are ○○○○○○○ or 7 circles in box B.

16. *(c)* From given figure, 11 flowers are there in bag 2.

17. *(c)*   Bag 1   Bag 2   Bag 3
   11 flowers   11   12

Total flowers are there in all the bags
= 11 + 11 + 12 = 34

18. *(a)* From question (17) Bag 1 and Bag 2 have the same number of flowers.

19. *(b)* Given abacus

? = $\boxed{4}$ tens and 5 ones + 2 tens and 3 ones

$$\begin{array}{r} 45 \\ +\quad 23 \\ \hline 68 \end{array}$$

= 45 + 23 or

∴ ? = 68

20. *(c)* $23 + 14 =$

$$\begin{array}{r} 23 \\ + \ 14 \\ \hline 37 \end{array}$$

Hence, option (c) is correct answer.

21. *(b)* $? = \boxed{1 \text{ ten} + 3 \text{ ones}} + \boxed{2 \text{ tens } 3 \text{ ones}}$

$= 13 + 23$

$$= \begin{array}{r} 13 \\ + \ 23 \\ \hline 36 \end{array}$$

22. *(a)*

$$\begin{array}{c} 7 \text{ tens} \\ 8 \text{ ones} \end{array} + \begin{array}{c} 2 \text{ tens} \\ 1 \text{ one} \end{array} = \begin{array}{r} 78 \\ + \ 21 \\ \hline 99 \end{array} \text{ or } 9 \text{ ten } 9 \text{ ones}$$

and

23. *(b)* $? = \boxed{11} + \boxed{0} = 11$

24. *(c)* 4 steps + 5 steps = 9 (to see the number line)

25. *(c)* According to the question,

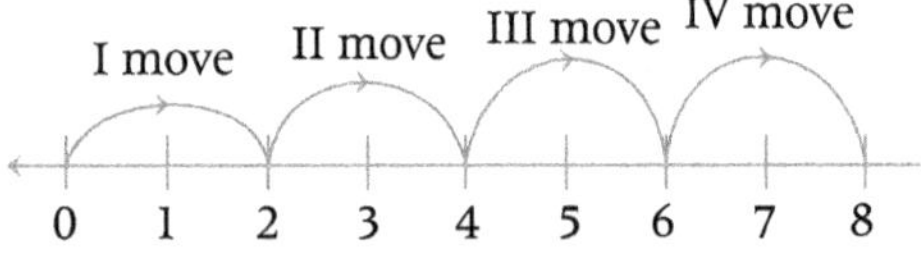

Hence, option (c) is correct answer.

26. *(a)* Option (a)

$$7 + 2 \boxed{=} 4 + 5$$
$$9 \qquad\quad 9$$

In option (b), (c) and (d) sign "=" can not be placed.

27. *(d)*

In (a)
$$\begin{array}{r} 7 \\ + \ 5 \\ \hline 12 \end{array}$$

In (b)
$$\begin{array}{r} 3 \\ + \ 7 \\ \hline 10 \end{array}$$

In (c)
$$\begin{array}{r} 8 \\ + \ 3 \\ \hline 11 \end{array}$$

In (d)
$$\begin{array}{r} 6 \\ + \ 7 \\ \hline 13 \end{array}$$

So, 13 or D is the greatest.

28. *(c)* In (A), $4 + 5 + 6 = |||| + ||||| + |||||| = 15$

In (B), $3 + 7 + 2 = ||| + ||||||| + || = 12$

In (C), $8 + 8 + 2 = |||||||| + ||||||||+ || = 18$

Sum, greatest to smallest is C, A, B.

29. *(c)* According to the grid,

$$? = \begin{array}{r} 4 \\ + \ 4 \\ \hline 8 \end{array}$$

3. Subtraction

1. *(b)*
$$\begin{array}{r} 10 \\ - \ 6 \\ \hline 4 \end{array}$$

2. *(a)*
$$\begin{array}{r} 6 \\ - \ 2 \\ \hline 4 \end{array} \text{ or }$$

3. *(a)*
$$\begin{array}{r} 5 \\ - \ 2 \\ \hline 3 \end{array} \text{ or }$$

4. *(d)*
$$\begin{array}{r} 7 \\ - \ 3 \\ \hline 4 \end{array}$$

5. *(b)*
$$\begin{array}{r} \text{Total Fruits} = 8 \\ \text{Cut Fruits} = 3 \\ \hline \text{Uncut Fruits} = 5 \end{array}$$

6. *(c)*
$$\begin{array}{r} \text{Total softies} = 12 \\ \text{uncrossed softies} = 4 \\ \hline \text{Crossed softies} = 8 \end{array}$$

7. *(b)*
$$\begin{array}{r} \text{Ali had ducks} = 12 \\ \text{Died ducks} = 4 \\ \hline \text{Left ducks with Ali} = 8 \end{array}$$

8. *(b)* $? = \begin{array}{r} 48 \\ - \ 12 \\ \hline 36 \end{array}$ and

9. (c)

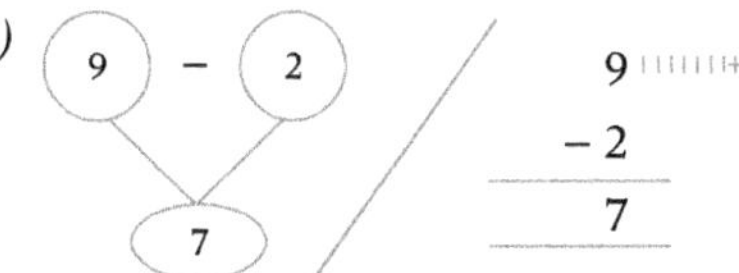

$$9 - 2 = 7$$

$$\begin{array}{r} 9 \\ -\,2 \\ \hline 7 \end{array}$$

10. (a)

$$? = \begin{array}{r} 10 \\ -\,3 \\ \hline 7 \end{array}$$

option (a)

$$\begin{array}{r} 8 \\ -\,1 \\ \hline 7 \end{array} \text{ correct}$$

Option (b), (c), (d) are not same as 7.

11. (c)

$$? = \begin{array}{r} 53 \\ -\,42 \\ \hline 11 \end{array} \text{ and}$$

So, option (c) is correct answer.

12. (c)

Ankit has toffee $= 10$
Ankit eats toffee $= 3$
Ankit has left toffee $= 7$ or $10 - 3 = 7$

13. (c)

A book has the pages $= 66$
Vinya read the pages $= 35$ and
Left pages $= 31$

14. (c)

From option (a)
$$\begin{array}{r} 29 \\ -\,14 \\ \hline 15 \end{array} \text{ (not correct)}$$

From option (b)
$$\begin{array}{r} 25 \\ -\,12 \\ \hline 13 \end{array} \text{ (not correct)}$$

From option (c)
$$\begin{array}{r} 37 \\ -\,11 \\ \hline 26 \end{array} \text{ and (correct)}$$

From option (d)
$$\begin{array}{r} 22 \\ -\,10 \\ \hline 12 \end{array} \text{ (not correct)}$$

15. (c) Correct difference
$$\begin{array}{r} 79 \\ -\,54 \\ \hline 25 \end{array} \text{ and}$$

16. (a) $? =$ Seventeen – Four
$$= \begin{array}{r} 17 \\ -\,4 \\ \hline 13 \end{array} \text{ or Thirteen}$$

17. (a)
$$\begin{array}{r} 9 \\ -\,4 \\ \hline 5 \end{array}$$

Hence, 5 should be subtracted.

18. (a)
$$\begin{array}{r} 27 \\ -\,21 \\ \hline 6 \end{array}$$

Here, option (a) shows 6 or $27 - 21 = 6$.

19. (a)
$$\begin{array}{r} 47 \\ -\,32 \\ \hline 15 \end{array}$$

Here, option (a) shows 15 or $47 - 32 = 15$

20. (b) Ali reach now $= 5$ (from number line)

21. (c) Option (c) represented 3 less than 10.

or
$$\begin{array}{r} 10 \\ -\,3 \\ \hline 7 \end{array}$$

22. (a)

Total students $= 84$
Number of girls $= 42$ and
Number of boys $= 42$

23. (b)

$$\triangle - | = 15 - 12$$

$$\begin{array}{r} 15 \\ -\,12 \\ \hline 3 \end{array}$$

24. *(a)* Number of bats = 12

Number of balls = 5

∴ Required number   12
     −   5
       7

25. *(a)*

? = (9 tens, 3 ones) − (6 tens, 2 ones)

= 93 − 62

or   93
   − 62
    31   or 3 tens 1 one

26. *(c)* Here, the greatest number = 72

and the smallest number = 11

∴ Required difference   72
       − 11   and
        61

27. *(c)* According to the grid ? =
     4
  − 2
    2

4. Measurement

1. *(b)* The key of option (b) is the longest key.

2. *(a)* The ice-cream of option (a) is the biggest ice-cream.

3. *(c)* The kite of option (c) has the shortest tail.

4. *(c)* S hammer is longer than hammer R.

5. *(b)*

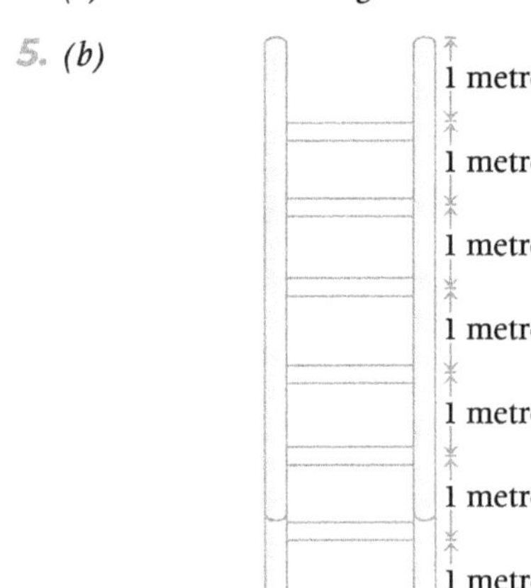

∴ Length of the ladder is 7 metres.

6. *(a)*

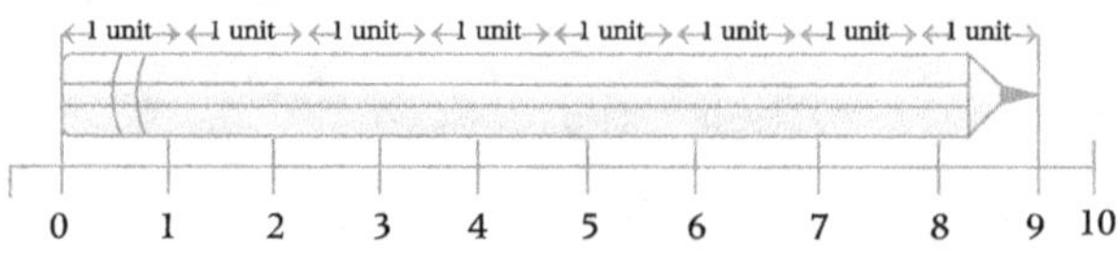

∴ Length of pencil = 8 units

Solutions (7-10)

Length of pencil A = 5 units

Length of pencil B = 3 units

Length of pencil C = 6 units

Length of pencil D = 8 units

7. *(d)* The longest pencil is D.

8. *(b)* The smallest pencil is B.

9. *(b)* Pencil B is shorter than pencil C = Length of pencil C − Length of pencil B

= 6 − 3 = 3 units

10. *(b)* The length of pencil D = 8 units

11. *(a)* From figure, *P* butterfly is at the greatest distance from the wall.

12. *(a)* From figure distance between tree *A* and tree *B* is 10 m.

13. *(b)* According to the question,

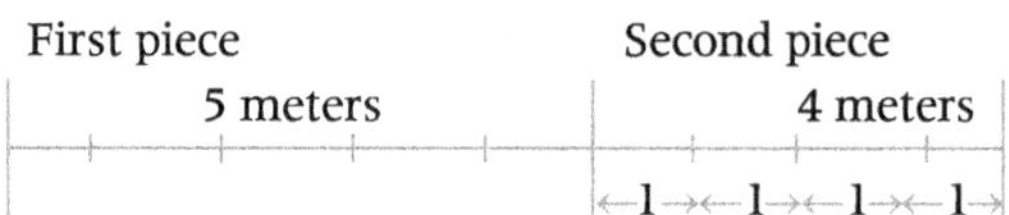

∴ The length of new rope = 5 + 4 = 9 m

14. *(b)* From figure, candle S is bigger than candle Q but shorter than candle P.

14. *(b)* From figure, candle S is bigger than candle Q but shorter than candle P.

Solutions (15-17)

Weight of box A = 4 kg

Weight of box B = 4 kg + 4 kg = 8 kg

Weight of box C = 2 kg

15. *(b)* The box B is heaviest.

16. *(c)* The box C is lightest.

17. *(b)* Box B weights, more than box C = Weight of box B – Weight of box C

$$\begin{array}{r} 8 \\ -\ 2 \\ \hline 6 \ \text{kg} \end{array}$$

18. *(c)* The car is heaviest among the TV, flower and book.

19. *(c)* Picture C shows that ball 1 is lighter than ball 2 because balance up of ball 1 side.

20. *(b)* Bat is heavier than the ball.

21. *(b)* We see the balance that 3 apples weighs as much as 4 mangoes.

22. *(b)* From the figure of balance, the heavier object is a book balance down of book side.

23. *(b)* Weight of Box = $\Delta + \Delta + \Delta + \Delta + \Delta + \Delta$
= 1gm + 1gm + 1gm + 1gm + 1gm + 1gm
= 6 gm

24. *(b)* From the figure of balance.

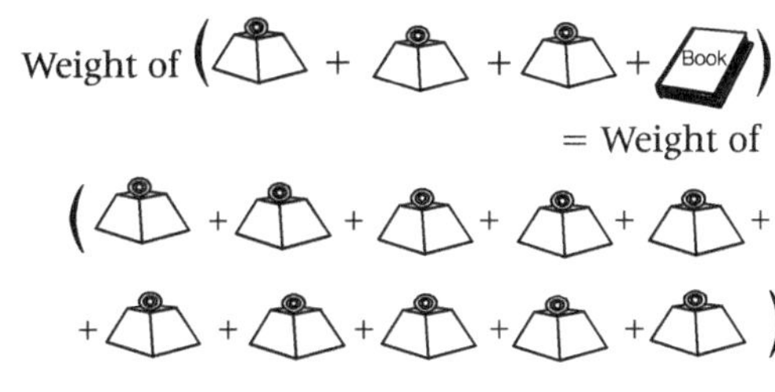

∴ Weight of Book = weight of

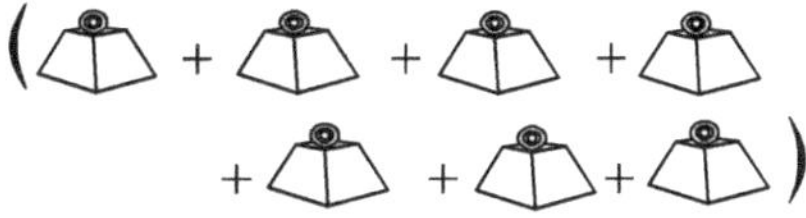

= 1 unit + 1 unit + 1 unit + 1 unit
+ 1 unit + 1 unit + 1 unit
= 7 units

25. *(b)* Increase in weight of Reena =

$$\begin{array}{r} 40 \\ -\ 20 \\ \hline 20 \ \text{kg} \end{array}$$

26. *(c)* Bucket of option (c) has the least quantity of water in it.

27. *(d)* Bottle of option (d) can hold more quantity sanitizer.

28. *(b)* The jug can hold juice
= 1 litre + 1 litre + 1 litre + 1 litre
= 4 litre

5. Money

1. *(b)* Total money = ₹ 1 + ₹ 2 + ₹ 2 + ₹ 5 + ₹ 5
(or । +॥ +॥ +॥॥॥ +॥॥॥)
= ₹ 15

2. *(b)* Meen has = ₹ 10 + ₹ 1 + ₹ 1 + ₹ 2 + ₹ 5
= ₹ 19
Her father gave = ₹ 1 + ₹ 2 + ₹ 5 + ₹ 10
= ₹ 18
Total money, Meena has now =

$$\begin{array}{r} 19 \\ +\ 18 \\ \hline 37 \end{array}$$

or 37 = | ₹ 20 | ₹ 10 | ₹ 5 | ₹ 2 |

3. *(b)* ₹ 100 is the maximum cost. So, option (b) is correct answer.

4. *(c)* Cost of flower is = ₹ 5

∴ Cost of flowers
= ₹ 5 + ₹ 5 + ₹ 5 + ₹ 5 = ₹ 20

5. *(b)* Amount shown in option (a)
= ₹ 10 + ₹ 20 = ₹ 30 is greater than ₹ 20.
Amount shown in option (b)
= ₹ 10 + ₹ 5 + ₹ 1 = ₹ 16 is less than ₹ 20.
Amount shown in option (c)
= ₹ 5 + ₹ 5 + ₹ 10 + ₹ 10
= ₹ 30, is greater than ₹ 20.
Amount shown in option (d)
= ₹ 50 is greater than ₹ 20

6. *(b)* Ankit has the money = ₹ 10
He spend for chips = ₹ 5

The money left with him = ₹ 5

7. *(c)*
$$\begin{array}{r} \text{Rohan gave money} = ₹\,50 \\ \text{Cost of toy car} \; = ₹\,40 \\ \hline \text{He will get back the money} = ₹\,10 \end{array}$$

8. *(a)*
$$\begin{array}{r} \text{Purnima has the money} = ₹\,50 \\ \text{She spend for apples} = ₹\,30 \\ \hline \text{Money is left with her} = ₹\,20 \end{array}$$

9. *(b)* Money shown in option (a)
$$= ₹\,10 + ₹\,10 + ₹\,20 + ₹\,10$$
$$= ₹\,50, \text{ is not more than } ₹\,100$$
Money shown in option (b)
$$= ₹\,10 + ₹\,50 + ₹\,50 + ₹\,20$$
$$= ₹\,130, \text{ is more than } ₹\,100$$
Money shown in option (c)
$$= ₹\,2 + ₹\,10 + ₹\,10$$
$$= ₹\,22, \text{ is not more than } ₹\,100$$
Money shown in option (d)
$$= ₹\,10 + ₹\,20 + ₹\,1 + ₹\,2$$
$$= ₹\,33, \text{ is not more than } ₹\,100$$
Hence, option (b) is correct answer.

10. *(c)* Money shown in option (a) $= ₹\,1 + ₹\,1 = ₹\,2$
Money shown in option (b) $= ₹\,2 + ₹\,2 = ₹\,4$
Money shown in option (c)
$$= ₹\,1 + ₹\,2 + ₹\,5 = ₹\,8$$
Money shown in option (d)
$$= ₹\,10 + ₹\,2 + ₹\,1 + ₹\,2 = ₹\,15$$
Hence, option (c) is correct answer.

11. *(c)* Money shown in option (a)
$$= ₹\,2 + ₹\,2 + ₹\,2 = ₹\,6$$
Money shown in option (b)
$$= ₹\,1 + ₹\,1 + ₹\,1 = ₹\,3$$
Money shown in option (c)
$$= ₹\,2 + ₹\,1 + ₹\,2 = ₹\,5$$
Money shown in option (d)
$$= ₹\,5 + ₹\,10 + ₹\,1 = ₹\,16$$
Hence, correct exchange of ₹ 5 is in option (c).

12. *(a)* Money shown in option (a)
$$= ₹\,10 + ₹\,10 + ₹\,20 = ₹\,40$$
Money shown in option (b)
$$= ₹\,5 + ₹\,5 + ₹\,5 = ₹\,15$$

Money shown in option (c)
$$= ₹\,2 + ₹\,5 + ₹\,10 = ₹\,17$$
Money shown in option (d)
$$= ₹\,10 + ₹\,2 + ₹\,1 = ₹\,13$$
Hence, money for doll ₹ 40 in option (a).

13. *(a)* Cost of 1 teddy bear $= ₹\,20$
Cost of 2 teddy bear $= ₹\,20 + ₹\,20 = ₹\,40$
Hence, 2 teddy bear can be bought for ₹ 40.

14. *(b)*
$$\begin{array}{r} \text{Raghav has} \; = ₹\,50 \\ \text{he pays for ball} = ₹\,20 \\ \hline \text{left money} \; = ₹\,30 \end{array}$$

So, he can purchase

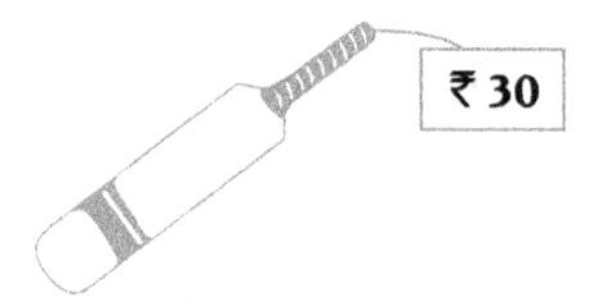

15. *(c)* Rahul has $= ₹\,90$
Here, cost of a toy ₹ 75 is less than ₹ 90, cost of a doll ₹ 100, a toy car ₹ 120, and a pencil box ₹ 95 are more than ₹ 90.
Hence, he can buy a toy ₹ 75.

16. *(c)* Cost of 1 carrot $= ₹\,2$
Cost of 3 carrots $= ₹\,2 + ₹\,2 + ₹\,2 = ₹\,6$

17. *(a)* I pay to buy a potato $= ₹\,5$

18. *(b)*
$$\begin{array}{r} \text{Cost of 1 brinjal} \; = ₹\,6 \\ \text{Cost of 1 tomato} \; = ₹\,4 \\ \hline \text{pay more for brinjal} \\ \text{than a tomato} \; = ₹\,2 \end{array}$$

19. *(c)* From (A), money
$$= ₹\,10 + ₹\,10 + ₹\,10 + ₹\,10 = ₹\,40$$
$$[\text{Match} \rightarrow (\text{iii})]$$
From (B), money $= ₹\,50 + ₹\,20 + ₹\,5 + ₹\,5$
$$= ₹\,80 \; [\text{Match} \rightarrow (\text{iv})]$$
From (C), money
$$= ₹\,10 + ₹\,20 + ₹\,20 = ₹\,50 \; [\text{Match} \rightarrow (\text{i})]$$
From (D),
$$\text{money} = ₹\,50 + ₹\,50 = ₹\,100 \; [\text{Match} \rightarrow (\text{ii})]$$
So, A—iii, B—iv, C—i, D—ii, i.e. option (c) is correct answer.

20. *(b)* Ankit saved = ₹ 10 + ₹ 5 + ₹ 2 = ₹ 17

Shubham saved = ₹ 1 + ₹ 1 = ₹ 2

Aaryan saved = ₹ 5 + ₹ 1 = ₹ 6

Mohit saved = ₹ 2 + ₹ 2 + ₹ 2 + ₹ 1 = ₹ 7

Hence, Shubham saved the less amount.

21. *(b)*

Cost of book = ₹ 80

Seema has = ₹ 50

She needs to by the book = ₹ 30

22. *(b)* Bottle has the lowest amount ₹ 25.

23. *(b)*

Cost of a lunch box = ₹ 40

Cost of a bottle = ₹ 25

The bill paid by him = ₹ 65

6. Time

1. *(b)* 12 O'clock in the night is called mid-night.

2. *(b)* The time is 4 O'clock. [shown the clock]

3. *(c)* The long hand takes 5 min to move from 2 to 3.

4. *(b)* The long has is pointing at 30 min.

5. *(a)* Time 2 h after 4 O'clock will be = 6 O'clock.

Here, option (a) clock is showing 6 O'clock.

6. *(b)* The clock is showing at 12 of hour hand.

∴ After 12 h, the hour hand will be on 12, because the hour hand complete one round for 12 h.

7. *(a)* Sheela started playing at 3 : 00 pm.

Time 3 : 00 pm to 4 : 00 pm = 1 h

Time 4 : 00 pm to 4 : 30 pm = 30 min

∴ The time taken by Sheela = 3 : 00 to 4 : 30 pm = 1 h 30 min

8. *(c)* Ram goes out for morning walk

= 6 O'clock

Time come back home

= after 1 hour of 6 O'clock

= 7 O'clock

9. *(c)* We take breakfast at morning. So, option (a) breakfast at 2 O'clock in the night, is not correct.

- We are not sleeping at 6 O'clock in the evening. So, option (b) is not correct.

- We are going to school at 7 O'clock in the morning. So, option (c) is correct.

- We are not bathing at 5 O'clock in the evening. So, option (d) is not correct.

10. *(b)* We know that 1 h has 60 min.

∴ 2 h have = 60 min + 60 min

11. *(c)* Ascending order of time

5, 10, 15, 25

Ishu, Chirag, Shivam, Ankit

∴ Shivam will be third to reach school.

12. *(d)* 7 days are there in a week.

13. *(b)* Name of days of a week in order are following.

Monday, Tuesday, Wednesday, Thursday, Friday, Saturday, Sunday

So, Wednesday comes after Tuesday.

14. *(b)*

Yesterday ←$\xleftarrow{\text{before}}$ Today $\xrightarrow{\text{after}}$ Tomorrow

↓　　　　　　↓　　　　　↓

Friday　　　Saturday　　Sunday

15. *(d)* 12 months are there in a year.

16. *(a)* We know that the number of days of the following months.

January, March, May, July, August, October, December ⟶ 31 days

April, June, September, November ⟶ 30 days

February ⟶ 28 or 29 days

∴ 31 days are in July month.

17. *(b)* We know that the name of months in order are following.

1st	2nd	3rd	4th
January,	February,	March,	April,

5th	6th	7th	8th	9th
May,	June,	July,	August,	September

10th	11th	12th
October,	November,	December

∴ July month comes just after sixth month (or June) of a year.

18. *(a)* <u>November</u> comes after July and before December.

[See the order of months in Q. 17]

19. *(b)* From given calendar, 5 Tuesday are there in the given month.

20. *(b)* Date of today is 9th.

Rohan's birthday is on the 12th.

∴ 3 days are left for Rohan's birthday.

21. *(c)* From given calendar third Saturday falls on 20th date of the given month.

22. *(b)* The last day of the month is Wednesday.

23. *(d)* Gopal's birthday is in February.

30 Feb, his birthday cannot fall, because the maximum number of days on February are 28 and 29 days (28 days in ordinary year and 29 days in a leap year).

24. *(b)* A leap year has 366 days. (While a ordinary year has 365 days).

7. Shapes

1. *(a)* D consist of straight line and curved line both.

2. *(c)* Write name in the given figure.

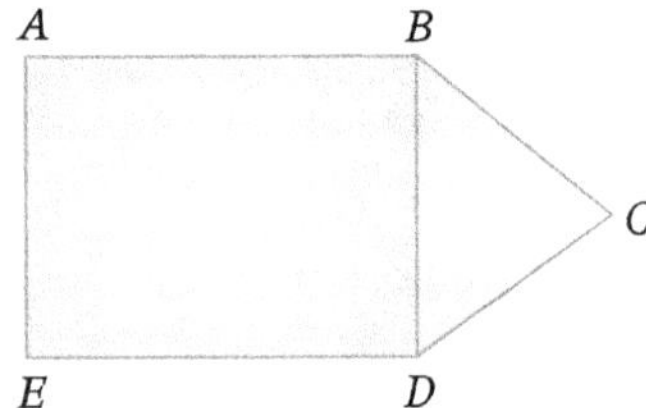

There are straight line *AB*, *BC*, *CD*, *BD*, *ED*, *AE* i.e. 6 straight lines are there in given figure.

3. *(b)* Option (b) shape is a cylinder.

4. *(b)* Option (b) shape is a sphere.

5. *(b)* Cone is the shape of a softy.

6. *(a)* Pepsi cane is in cylinder shape.

7. *(a)* Option (a) shape of circle.

8. *(b)* Option (b) is a cuboid from the given figure.

9. *(a)* Rectangle is not shown in the box.

10. *(b)* Cylinder and sphere kept on the table.

[2 cylinder and 2 sphere kept on the table]

11. *(d)* The shape of the shaded region is a square.

12. *(c)* Circle is not shown in the given figure.

13. *(b)* Option (a) figure is a cube, it is not a circle (not matched)

Option (b) figure is a sphere, (matched correctly)

Option (c) figure is a cone, it is not a cylinder. (not matched)

Option (d) figure is a cuboid, it is not a cone. (not matched)

14. *(d)*

	Shape	Name
(a)	◯	Circle (iv)
(b)	△	Triangle (iii)
(c)	▭	Rectangle (ii)
(d)	▱	Cuboid (i)

Hence, option (d) is correct answer.

15. *(a)* A triangle has 3 sides.

16. *(a)* A rectangle has 4 corner.

17. *(c)* Option (c) is the odd one out because triangle has 3 sides other shapes has 4 sides.

18. *(b)* Option (b) shape has 3 corners.

19. *(c)* In the given figure

1 → Triangle, 1 → Circle, 1 → Square

∴ Total number of shapes in the following figure = 3

20. *(b)* 3 triangles are present in the box.

21. *(d)* 1 rectangle, 5 triangles shown in the given figure.

22. *(a)* Shapes P and Q will combine to form a cone.

23. *(a)* 17 rectangles are present in the given figure.

8. Patterns

1. *(b)* This pattern as

Cake → Robot → Cake → Robot

∴ ? = 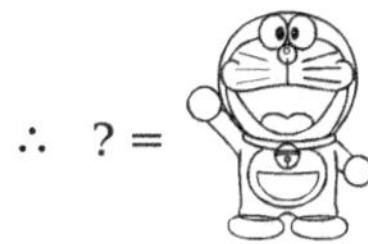

2. *(c)* This pattern as, the direction of the arrow is being opposite in next pattern.

∴ ? = 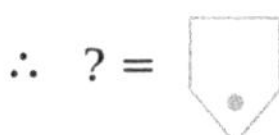

3. *(c)* The pattern as

Circle, Triangle, Rectangle in each next pattern.

∴ Fill in blank figure =

4. *(a)* This pattern as

(Dot, Triangle, Square) in each next pattern.

∴ ? = 

5. *(a)* This pattern as 

in each next pattern.

∴ ? =

6. *(d)* This pattern as 4 leaves, 2 tomato in each next pattern.

∴ Next figure of this pattern =

7. *(d)* This pattern as 4 circles, 2 triangles in each next pattern.

∴? =

8. *(a)* This pattern as, 1 candy is increasing in each next pattern.

∴ Next pattern = 

9. *(c)* This pattern as, 1 star is increasing in each next pattern.

∴ ? = 

10. *(b)* This pattern as, 1 dot is increasing on the toy in each next pattern.

So, next pattern figure is

11. *(c)* This pattern as, 1 dot is increasing in box in each next pattern.

∴   ?   = 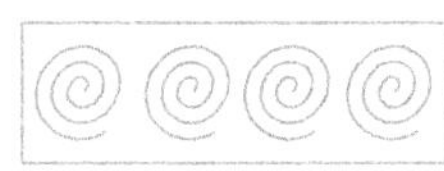

12. *(c)* This pattern as 1 (sprial) is increasing in box in each next pattern.

∴ Fill in the plane figure =

13. *(b)* This pattern as the figures comes alternative N and Z.

∴ ? = 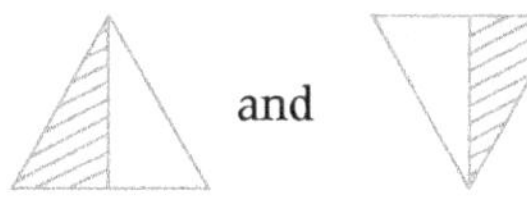

14. *(b)* This pattern as the figures comes alternative

 and

∴ ? =

15. (c) Suppose

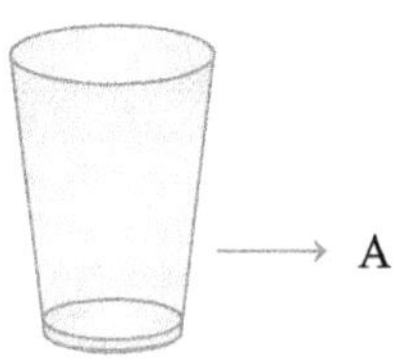

$\longrightarrow$ A

and

$\longrightarrow$ B

Then this pattern using letters = ABBB

16. (b) This pattern as AAA BBB CCC

∴ ? = CCC

17. (d) This pattern as

1 12 123 1234 12345

∴ ? = 12345

18. (a) This pattern as

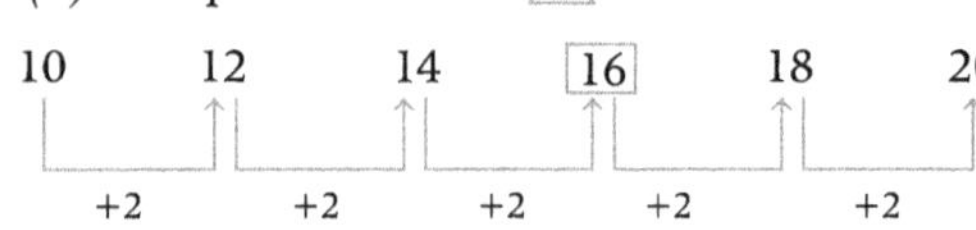

19. (c) This pattern as

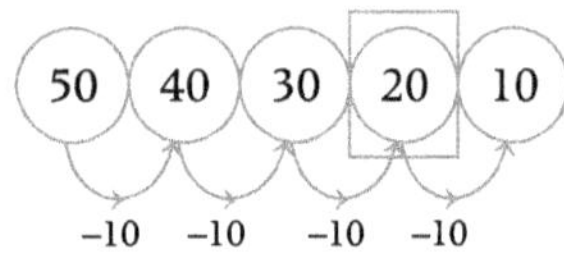

∴ 20 will come in the blank circle.

20. (b) This pattern as

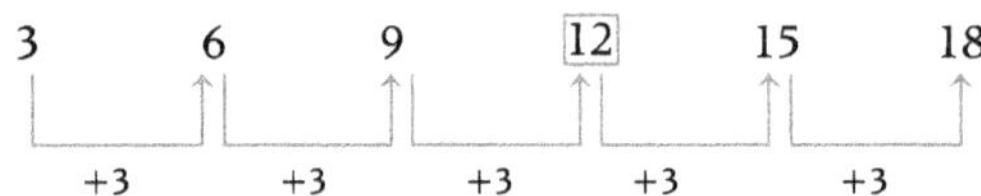

21. (b) This pattern as

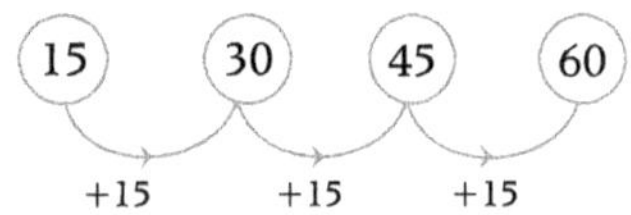

∴ ? = 45

22. (c) This pattern as

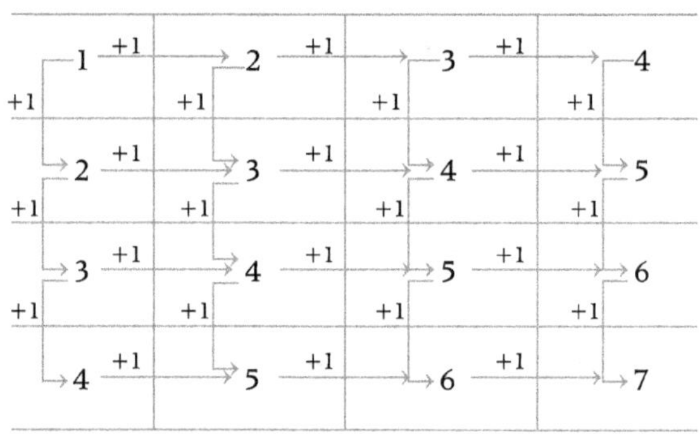

∴ The missing number

= 3456

23. (a) This pattern as

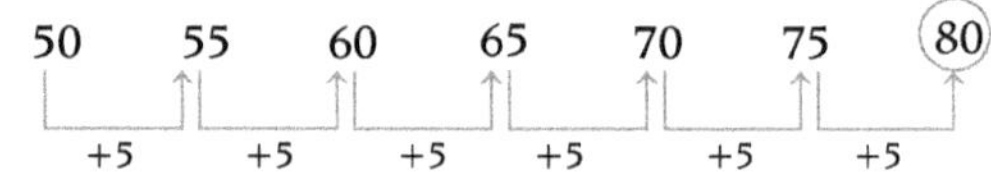

i.e. skip counting by 5

24. (c) In this pattern, the shaded part move 1 place in clockwise direction.

∴ ? = 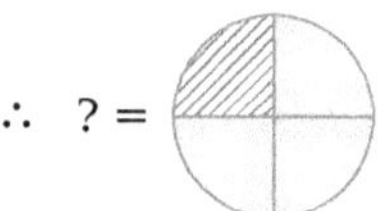

25. (c) This pattern as

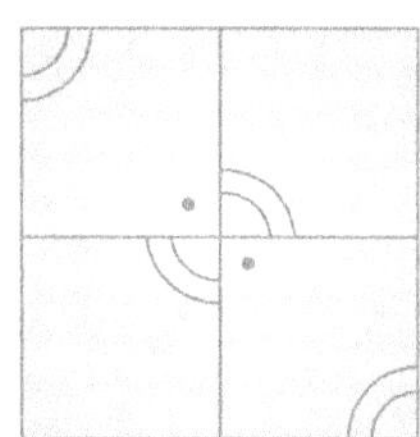

∴ ? =

9. Data Handling

Solutions (1-6)

Number of toys car = 4
Number of toys balls = 5
Number of toys racket = 5
Number of toys rings = 3
Number of toys pens = 2

1. *(b)* 'Pen' toy is least in number (or 2 pens)

2. *(c)* Balls and Rackets toys are same in number.

3. *(a)* 3 rings are there.

4. *(c)*

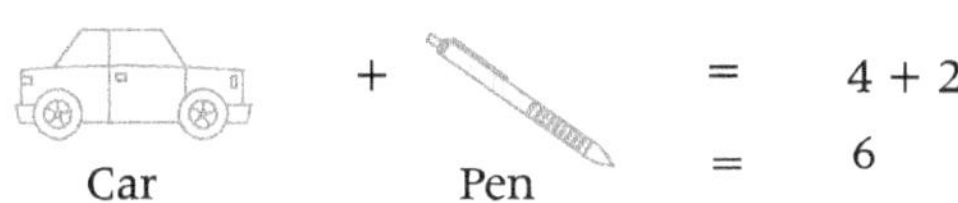

$$+ \quad = \quad 4 + 2$$
$$= \quad 6$$

5. *(b)* ∴ Required number = 5 – 3 = 2

6. *(a)* ∴ Required number = 5 – 4 = 1

Solutions (7-9)

Number of carrots = 8
Number of potatoes = 5
Number of mushrooms = 6
Number of brinjals = 4

7. *(b)* Difference between the number of carrots and mushrooms.
$$= 8 – 6 = 2$$

8. *(b)* 5 potatoes are grown into the garden.

9. *(c)* 4 types of vegetables are grown by the farmer into his garden.

10. *(a)* Number of pineapples in figure 1 = 6.
Number of pineapples in figure 2 = 6
Number of pineapples in figure 3 = 5
Number of pineapples in figure 4 = 7
∴ 1 and 2 figures shows same number of pineapples.

Solutions (11-13)

Number of books read in Monday = 4
Number of books read in Tuesday = 5
Number of books read in Wednesday = 3
Number of books read in Thursday = 2
Number of books read in Friday = 4

11. *(c)* Number of books read in Wednesday = 3

12. *(d)* On Tuesday maximum books were read (i.e. 5 books).

13. *(c)* 2 books were read in 'Thursday'.

14. *(d)* Number of butterflies = 6
Number of frogs = 8
∴ Required difference = 8 – 6 = 2

Solutions (15 and 16)

Number of leaves collected by Max = 8
Number of leaves collected by Kajal = 6
Number of leaves collected by Vikram = 3
Number of leaves collected by Manish = 5
Number of leaves collected by Sonal = 9

15. *(d)* The number of leaves collected by Sonal
$$= 9$$

16. *(a)* Vikram collected the least number of leaves.

17. *(b)* The number of T-shirts = 4
The number of pants = 5
∴ Option (b) table shows the correct number of T-shirts and Pants.

18. *(a)* From given table, Shilpi has scored maximum marks. (i.e. 99 marks) in Mathematics.

19. *(d)* From given table, the marks of Dheeraj is 76.

Solutions (20-23)

Number of pencils were sold on Monday = 1
Number of pencils were sold on Tuesday = 3
Number of pencils were sold on Wednesday
$$= 2$$
Number of pencils were sold on Thursday = 4
Number of pencils were sold on Friday = 5

20. *(b)* Number of pencils were sold on Thursday
$$= 4$$

21. *(a)* The minimum number of pencils (i.e 1 pencil) were sold on "Monday".

22. *(d)* 2 pencils were sold on Wednesday.

23. *(b)* Total number of pencils sold from Monday to Wednesday = 1 + 3 + 2 = 6 pencils

74

Practice Set 1

1. *(c)* This pattern as, repeating the figures

◇ ☆ ⇧ in each next pattern.

∴ ? = ⇧

2. *(c)* Number of ◯ = 9

Number of ☆ = 5

∴ Required ☆ = 9 ‖‖‖‖‖‖
$$\begin{array}{r} 9 \\ -\ 5 \\ \hline 4 \end{array}$$

3. *(b)* Number of circles in the given figure = 9.

4. *(c)* This pattern as

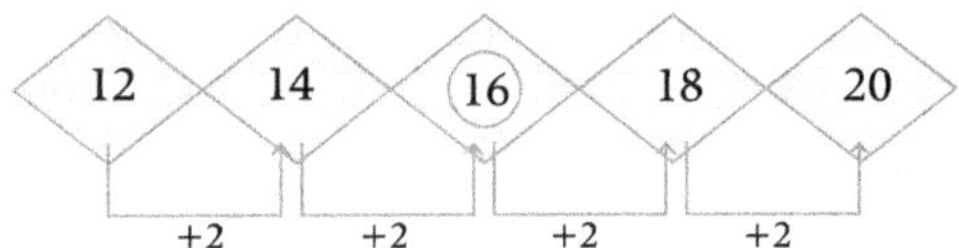

∴ ? = 16

5. *(c)*

$$\begin{array}{l} \text{Mother has potatoes } = 12 \\ \text{She uses potatoes } = \underline{\ 6\ } \\ \text{Potatoes are left } = 6 \end{array}$$

6. *(d)* This pattern as

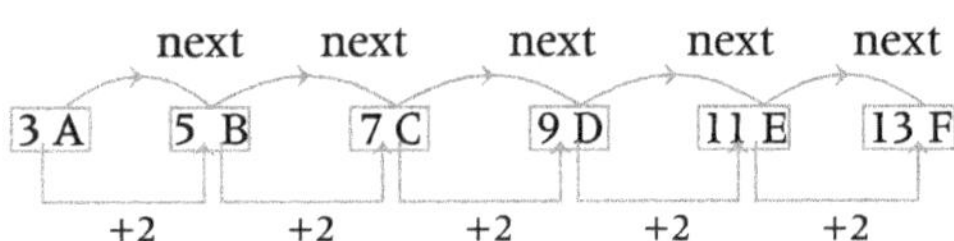

7. *(c)*

2 tens	3 ones	+	5 tens	1 one	=	?	4 ones

$$\begin{array}{r} 23 + 51 = 23 \\ +\ 51 \\ \hline 74 \end{array}$$ and

=

7 tens	4 ones

∴ ? = 7 tens.

8. *(d)*

Januray ⟵ last | Now February | ⟶ March

[∵ order of month of a yr is → January, February, March, April, May, June, July, August, September, October, November, December]

9. *(c)* Order of the day of a week is

Monday, Tuesday, Wednesday, Thursday, Friday, Saturday, Sunday.

∴ Saturday comes before Sunday.

10. *(a)*

$$\begin{array}{r} \text{Cost of ice-cream} = ₹10 \\ \text{Cost of two chocolates} = ₹10 \\ + \\ \hline \text{Total money Rahul needs} = ₹\,20 \end{array}$$

11. *(c)* The time is shown in the clock = 3 O'clock.

12. *(a)*

13. *(a)* From the given figure, 9 rectangles long is the pen.

14. *(c)* Number of lines in box (*A*) = 11

Number of lines in box (*B*) = 11

∴ Both box have equal lines.

15. (c) Option (c), total weight of *C* and *D*

$$\begin{array}{r} = 3\ \text{kg} \\ +\ 7\ \text{kg} \\ \hline 10\ \text{gk} \end{array}$$

16. *(c)* Weight of box is = 3 kg + 3kg + 3kg

= (‖‖ + ‖‖ + ‖‖) kg

= 9 kg

Solutions (Q. Nos. 17-20)

Number of toffees = 5

Number of ice-cream = 3

Number of balloons = 4

Number of car = 1

17. (c) Required number = 5 − 3 = 2

18. *(c)* Balloon is 4 in number.

19. *(d)* Total number of all the items are

= 5 + 3 + 4 + 1

= 13 (‖‖‖ + ‖‖ + ‖‖ + ‖)

20. *(b)* Balloons are more than ice-creams but less in numbers than toffees.

21. *(c)*   **22.** *(a)*

23. *(d)* The smallest number on candy $= 13$

The greatest number on candy $= 66$

$\therefore$ Required sum $=$
$$\begin{array}{r} 66 \\ + \ 13 \\ \hline 79 \end{array}$$ and

24. (b) Amount of option (b)
$$= ₹\,50 + ₹\,20 + ₹\,5 = ₹\,75$$

25. *(d)* The shape of ice-cream (softy) is a cone.

26. *(a)* Option (a), $5 - 3 = 2$, it is correct.

Option (b), $4 - 2 = 1$, it is not correct.
Option (c), $6 - 3 = 4$, it is not correct.
Option (d), $3 - 2 = 2$, it is not correct.

27. *(c)* P : $\underline{E}$ tree is the tallest. (P $\rightarrow E$)

Q : $\underline{C}$ tree is taller than tree A but shorter than E. (Q $\rightarrow C$)

Hence, option (c) is correct answer.

28. *(a)* The months of a yr have the number of days as the following

[January $\rightarrow 31$, February $\rightarrow 28$ or 29, March $\rightarrow 31$, April $\rightarrow 30$, May $\rightarrow 31$, June $\rightarrow 30$, July $\rightarrow 31$, August $\rightarrow 31$, September $\rightarrow 30$, October $\rightarrow 31$, November $\rightarrow 30$, December $\rightarrow 31$]

$\therefore$ In a yr September has 30 days.

29. *(c)* Cone is not present in the given cloud.

[circle, cylinder, rectangle are present].

30. *(c)*
$$\begin{array}{l} \text{Julee has the doll toys} = 37 \\ \text{Her sister gave her} = 11 \\ \hline \text{Total doll toys she have now} = 48 \end{array}$$

31. *(b)* Rajni had the biscuit $= 14$
$$\begin{array}{l} \text{She ate the biscuit} = 6 \\ \hline \text{Biscuit are left with her} = 8 \end{array}$$

32. *(b)* ? =

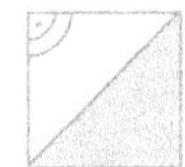

Hence, option (b) will complete the pattern.

33. *(c)* The number of triangles in the toy figure is $\underline{20}$.

34. *(d)* Parrot is the odd because parrot is a bird while all other are animals.

35. *(b)* (X) Total cost of a ball and a guitar
$$\begin{array}{r} ① \\ = \ ₹\,15 \\ + \ ₹\,45 \\ \hline ₹\,60 \end{array}$$ and $(X) \longrightarrow 3.$

(Y) Required amount $=$
$$\begin{array}{r} ₹\,75 \\ - \ ₹\,45 \\ \hline ₹\,30 \end{array}$$ or $(Y) \longrightarrow 1.$

(Z) Required amount $=$
$$\begin{array}{r} ₹\,15 \\ - \ ₹\,07 \\ \hline ₹\,8 \end{array}$$ or $(Z) \longrightarrow 2.$

Hence, $(X) \rightarrow 3, (Y) \rightarrow 1, (Z) \rightarrow 2$

Practice Set 2

1. *(b)* The time shown by the clock is 12 O' clock.

2. *(c)*   **3.** *(c)*

4. *(b)* Monday $\overset{\text{1st day}}{\rightarrow}$ Tuesday $\overset{\text{2nd day}}{\rightarrow}$ Wednesday $\overset{\text{3rd day}}{}$ $\overset{\text{4th day}}{\rightarrow}$ Thursday

5. *(c)*

6. (a) $? = ₹\,10 + ₹\,10 + ₹\,5$
$$\begin{array}{r} 10 \\ + \ 10 \\ \hline 20 \end{array}$$ and $$\begin{array}{r} 20 \\ + \ 05 \\ \hline 25 \end{array}$$
$= ₹\,25$

7. *(b)* These numbers as

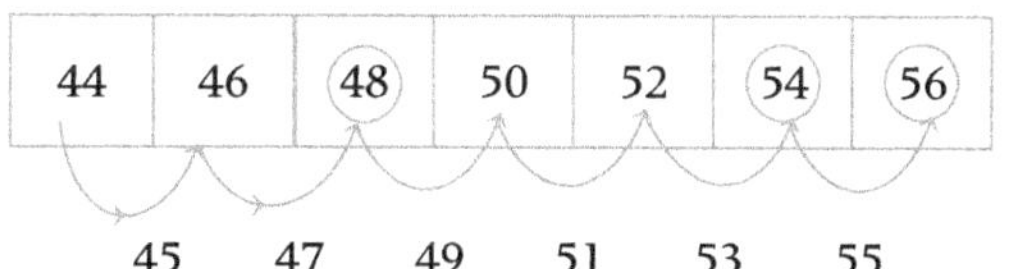

Hence, missing numbers $= 48, 54, 56$

8. *(a)* $6 + 5 =$
$$\begin{array}{r} 6 \\ + \ 5 \\ \hline 11 \end{array}$$

Here, 12 one of the number is more than $6 + 5$.

9. *(a)* 9 squares are there in the given figure.

10. *(c)* Option (c) coin 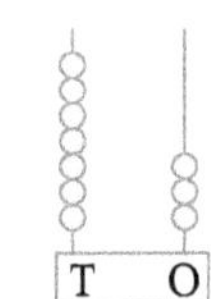 has the highest value.

11. *(b)* Option (b) Shape ◿ is in triangular shape.

12. *(a)* From the given abacus

? = 31 + 42

$$\begin{array}{r} 31 \\ + 42 \\ \hline 73 \end{array}$$

13. *(d)* The order of the day of a week, if

Sunday is the 1st day, is Sunday → Monday, Tuesday → Wednesday → Thursday → Friday → Saturday.

Hence, Saturday is the last day of week, if Sunday is the 1st day.

14. *(c)* Smith is on page number 20

∴ The next page number will be = 20 + 1 = 21 or 21 comes after 20.

15. *(c)* Number of children in a class = 28
Number of boys in a class = 12

Number of girls in a class = 16

16. *(a)* A : 17 − 15 = 17

$$\begin{array}{r} 17 \\ - 15 \\ \hline 2 \end{array} \rightarrow \text{Match (ii)}$$

B : 9 + 4 =

$$\begin{array}{r} 9 \\ + 4 \\ \hline 13 \end{array} \rightarrow \text{Match (iv)}$$

C : 15 − 0 = 15

$$\begin{array}{r} 15 \\ - 0 \\ \hline 15 \end{array} \rightarrow \text{Match (i)}$$

D : 8 + 3 =

$$\begin{array}{r} 8 \\ + 3 \\ \hline 11 \end{array} \rightarrow \text{Match (iii)}$$

Hence, A → (ii), B → (iv), C → (i), D → (iii)

17. *(a)* Cylinder is not present in the given figure.

18. *(d)* Option (d) shows the least value 20, because 31, 47 and 56 are greater than 20.

19. *(c)* This pattern as ($ $ ★ ★ ★) is reaction, in each next pattern.

∴ ? = ($ $)

20. *(c)* Joy has = ₹ 70

There is the cost of car is ₹ 70

∴ Joy can buy a car.

21. *(b)* is 4th, from the left end.

22. *(c)* Total numbers of balls = 9
Number of uncrossed balls = 6

Number of crossed balls = 3

23. *(c)* We count the flowers, then

The number of flowers are there altogether = 16 = 1 tens 6 ones.

24. *(c)* Watermelon is the heavier than mango, brinjal and biscuit.

25. *(d)* Option (d) activity is correct because the lunch time, 1 O'clock noon is correct.

26. *(b)* Pragya starts her coaching class on 2nd Monday.

From the clander, date of 2nd Monday is 12th. Hence, Pragya start her coaching class on 12th July.

27. *(b)* Name of the trees from the tallest to the shortest is *R, P, S, Q, T*

28. *(a)*

29. *(d)* We see the given figure, the shape of the can is cylinder.

30. *(b)*

Number of  are there in the picture is = 5

31. *(a)* **32.** *(c)*

33. *(b)* As,

Same as

34. *(a)* **35.** *(c)*